Some of Cornwall's earliest ports were established inland, at or near the heads of navigation of rivers, rendering themselves less prone to raids from the sea and giving better access to the hinterland at a time when land transport was almost impractical for large loads. Such ports were Saltash on the River Tamar, Lostwithiel on the River Fowey, Tregony and Truro on the Fal Estuary, Helston on the River Cober and Lelant on the Hayle river. As the threat of attack diminished over the centuries, so too did the salt water in

The riverfront and limekilns at Lostwithiel

some of these places: the river at Lostwithiel silted and the channel became shallow – in inverse proportion to ships, which were becoming bigger and deeper; the tide which once reached Tregony began to recede as long ago as the middle ages; and Helston was isolated from the sea when the shingle of the Loe Bar formed a barrier across the Cober's mouth. The increasing size of ocean going shipping, also restricted navigation to inland ports like Truro and Wadebridge.

Ports and harbours at estuary mouths, such as Looe, Fowey, Falmouth and Padstow, and in sheltered coastal locations like Penzance and St Ives, thus came to prominence and were well placed for the growth of maritime trade in the nineteenth century.

Brunel's Royal Albert Bridge of 1859 and the Tamar Suspension Bridge of 1961 at Saltash

SALTASH. A port since the twelfth century, exporting tin from Dartmoor, Saltash was eclipsed in the thirteenth century by Plymouth. However, it held jurisdiction over the entire Tamar estuary until this largely symbolic 'authority' was abolished in 1835. Little remains of the town's maritime heritage today, other than its proximity to the waters' edge. The maritime quarter of Saltash, known as Waterside, and virtually all of the older waterside features have been demolished. However, the waterfront is worth a visit, offering a spectacular view of Brunel's Royal Albert Bridge, the Tamar Suspension Bridge and

the Saltash reach of the River Tamar. The floating bridge slipway of the ancient Saltash Ferry, which was replaced by the suspension bridge in 1961, is still evident, as are parts of the former Passage House Inn – now renamed The Boatman Inn .

LOSTWITHIEL. Established as a port for Bodmin, Lostwithiel was one of the county's foremost ports from the twelfth to the mid-fourteenth century, after which silt from tin streaming works began to choke the River Fowey. Lostwithiel continued to collect keelage and anchorage dues from ships in the river until the Fowey Harbour Board was established in 1870. Lostwithiel's privilege of holding a marine court is still symbolised by the town's use of a miniature silver oar as one of its maces.

Agricultural barge traffic continued right up to the beginning of the twentieth century and evidence of this period survives in a bank of limekilns and riverside buildings downstream of the fifteenth century bridge over the Fowey. An evening visit is usually rewarded with parking space near the bridge and a pleasant hour or so pottering along the riverbank. The town's quays now seem hopelessly un-navigable but can still be reached by small powered boats.

TREGONY. A medieval port until the tide began receding during the fifteenth century. Some evidence suggests that the River Fal might have been navigable even further upstream to a place near the present day Golden Mill. Until 1740, when the Sett Bridge was built over the Fal near Ruan Lanihorne, the river was navigable to Penvose Quay.

PENRYN. At the head of navigation on the Penryn river, Penryn was a medieval victualling port which once held jurisdiction over the entire stretch of water that is now Falmouth Harbour. While Penryn's importance as a Port Authority ended in 1652, when the Customs House was removed to the developing harbour of Smithwick (later renamed Falmouth), its maritime commerce continued well into the twentieth century. Trade at Penryn during the nineteenth and twentieth centuries included the export of granite from the nearby Freemans' quarries, and the unusual import trade of live cattle from Corunna – until public concern regarding the animals' welfare forced its end. Until the middle of the last century ketches and barges served the nearby agricultural community and landed coal supplies for local use.

Penryn's past as a trading port is evident from extensive warehousing and quayside facilities and in the continued use of quayside warehouses – albeit now served from the main Falmouth road rather than the river.

ST MICHAEL'S MOUNT. This spectacular island is linked to Marazion by a causeway and boasts its own harbour. The first pier, having been built during the fifteenth century, offered security from attack both from the land and sea – the latter by cannon high up on the mount. In 1727 the St Aubyn family extended the pier and improved the harbour and a century later the pier was extended again. Salt fish, tin and copper ore were

The harbour and ferryboats on St Michael's Mount

transported by packhorse over the causeway for export from the harbour. Imports included coal, iron, timber and corn.

Lord St Leven still resides on the Mount, but it is owned by the National Trust. Two of the nineteenth century rowing barges, which were used as ferries (in which the family were rowed by liveried watermen) have survived and can usually be found in the harbour or out of the water on the quayside.

On the piers are to be seen old cannon barrels used as bollards, while on the east pier is the footprint of Queen Victoria, in cement, commemorating her visit to the Mount in 1846. St Michael's Mount can be visited by crossing the causeway at low tide, or by ferry.

The Quay. Penryn.

Penryn c1900

Centuries ago, when land transport was by horse and wagon on unsurfaced roads, water transport had many advantages – as demonstrated by the eighteenth century development of inland waterways. In a remote peninsula such as Cornwall the sea was the natural means of communication with the rest of the kingdom, as well as with more distant lands – few parts of the county were more than a dozen or so miles from the coast or from a navigable river.

Most Cornish ports and harbours supported fishing fleets, the products of the sea being an important part of the Cornishman's diet since prehistoric times. With increasing industrial activity many of these old granite piers and jetties were extended and engaged in the export of minerals – tin, copper and later, china clay, granite and slate. In most instances these activities continued alongside general local, continental and even worldwide, import and export trade. Each port involved in general trading also supported its locally owned – mostly locally built – merchant fleet. Such ports included Saltash, Looe, Fowey, Truro, Penryn, Falmouth, Penzance, St Ives, Portreath, Padstow, Boscastle and, for a relatively brief period during the nineteenth and twentieth centuries, Bude. The majority of these trading ports are located in the sheltered estuaries of the rivers Tamar, Looe, Fowey, Fal and Camel, or in bays protected from the prevailing south westerly winds such as St Austell Bay, Mounts Bay and St Ives Bay.

Wherever ships called to take out minerals, agricultural produce or fish, they imported coal, timber, salt, limestone and general goods. Shipping agents were appointed to handle the trade and charter vessels when necessary. Falmouth, being strategically located as a safe anchorage at the entrance of the English Channel, became an important port for sailing orders as agents like G. C. Fox and W. Broad advised ships' captains of their owners' sailing instructions, or arranged ('fixed') cargoes in other ports. Local merchant fleets were established, including the Stephens schooner fleet of Fowey, W. H. Lean of Falmouth, the Harveys of Hayle, D. W. Bain's schooners at Portreath, the fleet of Hitchens of St Agnes, and the later tramping steamers of the Chellew Steam Navigation Company of Truro and Edward Hain of St Ives. Entire communities owned shares in ships, at times beyond all proportion to the size of their harbour. Notable shipowning communities included:

Looe in the 1950s

GAFF CUTTER

KETCH

SCHOONER

TOPSAIL SCHOONER

BRIGANTINE

BARQUENTINE

BRIG

BARQUE

FULL RIGGED SHIP

The harbour at Newquay c1900

Calstock on the River Tamar – over a dozen miles from the open sea; Par in St Austell Bay; Newquay – where well over 100 vessels were owned at the peak of activity; Padstow – which supported 27 shipowning concerns in 1823; Port Isaac on the north coast; and Bude – where a mainly agricultural community, remote from any major town, owned a considerable fleet until early in the twentieth century.

The southern coast of Cornwall is blessed with sheltered bays and drowned river valleys (rias) forming deep water sounds – the Carrick Roadstead in the Fal estuary is acknowledged as one of the largest natural harbours in the world. Many of Cornwall's southern ports traded in tin during their early years. Penzance was a fishing harbour in Mounts Bay which became a coinage town and tin exporter during the nineteenth century. The port's general trade grew with successive harbour developments, which continued until the late nineteenth century.

The southern ports were particularly well placed for trade to the continent – both legal and otherwise. Privateering flourished at Fowey with the Mixtow family attacking French and Spanish ships in the English Channel under Royal Licence. Smuggling – or 'free trading' – evaded heavy taxation and was undertaken between various Cornish harbours and, in particular, the Channel Islands.

Fowey's trading prospects took an upward turn during the nineteenth century when china clay wharves were constructed immediately upstream from the town. The deep water harbour at Fowey lent itself to the establishment of merchant sailing fleets which engaged in the Newfoundland trade. This was based on carrying salted fish to the Mediterranean and salt back across to the small settlements on the coast of Newfoundland which survived by fishing for the plentiful cod in those waters. The largest fleet of schooners was owned by John Stephens and, quite typically, his small, fast and sea-worthy vessels were well suited to the salt fish trade – many benefited from the local builders' experience gained by an earlier need to outsail the Revenue cutters.

By the beginning of last century even these small fleets were feeling

Padstow

considerable economic pressures from the introduction of steam power and iron construction. Much trade, even locally, was being lost to shipping which was no longer so dependent on the weather and which carried larger cargoes, quicker than even the best west country schooner. These new vessels required a different kind of boatyard for their building and a much greater investment: with a few exceptions neither of these was available in Cornwall. The ageing sailing vessels hung on to some trade until after the Great War, where the need for speed, or the value of the cargo did not justify the change to steam. With auxiliary engines fitted others continued to work right up to the early 1960s, their longevity a tribute to the local shipwrights.

The southern ports were also convenient for shipping plying to the Baltic, the Mediterranean and the Atlantic. After its early history as a Post Office packet station for the Iberian Peninsula, the Caribbean, and North Atlantic, Falmouth was particularly well placed to profit from its role as the port for orders for ships in the English Channel, a role which faded when ship to shore radio communications were established during the early years of the twentieth century.

The geography of Cornwall's north coast did not lend itself to the establishment of large trading ports. The one substantial estuary of the River Camel is obstructed by sandbanks, formed by the dual action of tide and river flow. The port of Padstow and the river quays at Wadebridge enjoyed a period of success in the nineteenth century. But a decline in their mineral trade coupled with unfavourable navigation conditions has prevented any revival of the river's general trade.

St Ives is most closely associated with the fishing industry, but the port also attracted general trade, restricted however to beach landing, albeit protected by Smeaton's pier since 1770.

A succession of man made harbours were built at Hayle, Portreath, St Agnes, Newquay and Bude to cater initially for the mining, quarrying and agricultural industries. In the absence of any substantial natural alternative, these harbours also attracted general trade.

Sheltered sandy coves along the north coast lent themselves to potentially hazardous beach trading. Small coastal schooners, ketches and smacks came in to 'take the beach' as the tide receded. Vessels were developed with flatter hulls, similar to river barges, better suited for standing on a beach than for seaworthiness and speed on the open sea. Three of these inlets, Port Isaac, Port Gaverne and Boscastle exported Delabole slate and established their own small fleets of merchant vessels, trading mainly in the Irish Sea and the Bristol Channel.

Falmouth Docks from Flushing

Polruan

was built by the Brazen Island Shipyard of Polruan. Most of the Polruan waterfront upstream of Ferry Quay is still engaged in boatbuilding and yacht repair. The ship repair facilities of the Fowey Harbour Commissioners are located upstream, at the far end of the village.

A passenger ferry operates all year round, crossing the harbour from the end of Fore Street in Polruan to Whitehouse Slip in Fowey, offering a pleasant way to view Polruan from the water (and to get to Fowey).

Pont Pill

One of the best ways of exploring the maritime communities of Fowey Harbour is to spend a day on the Hall Walk, a circular route along the opposite tree lined bank of the harbour, using two ferries, which visits Polruan, Pont Pill, Bodinnick and Fowey and provides spectacular views of Fowey, Polruan and the coast to Dodman Point. Closer inspection of Fowey's waterfront can only be gained from the water itself.

POLRUAN. The village of Polruan lies just inside the mouth of the River Fowey. There is a mid nineteenth century coastguard watch house near the car park, at the top of the village. Polruan was a busy boat and ship building village; William Geach & Son built sloops and smacks until c1840, near the entrance of the harbour. The Slade family occupied a yard off West Street from 1856 until 1929. The hopper barge Lantic Bay – usually moored off Polruan or dredging in the Harbour –

PONT PILL. The quay at Pont, once frequented by ketches and barges, is owned by the National Trust and its limekiln, quay office and warehouse are carefully preserved, providing a good example of a Cornish agricultural community's river quay.

Fowey Harbour

Fowey's Troy class yachts

FOWEY. An ancient fishing hamlet, then medieval port, Fowey also became a centre for piracy. Mark Mixtow was one of the town's most notorious privateers. Licenced by the Crown to attack French ships, he extended this authority to include most shipping in the English Channel. The two blockhouses on either side of the river mouth once guarded the harbour and a chain could be pulled across the entrance. In the sixteenth century Fowey settled to general trading but the greatest change to the port's fortunes came late in the nineteenth century, with the construction of the clay wharves up-river, opposite Mixtow Pill.

As in most waterside cities and towns today, public access to the waterfront has become limited. The main public quays and slipways are to be found at Readymoney Cove – a sandy beach at the harbour mouth, and Whitehouse Slip – the landing place for the Polruan Ferry and notable for the distinctive harbour light, an iron structure of 1892, which dominates the view from the lane leading to the slip. Town Quay is very much the waterside centre of Fowey, from where boats run harbour trips, and self drive motor boats can be hired. At Albert Quay a pontoon landing serves Fowey Gallants yacht club and the swollen, summer season maritime community. It is also the berth for the Fowey Lifeboat (an RNLI shop is further along

North Street). To the north, Caffa Mill Pill, once the site of the Heller family's shipyard, is now filled in as a car park and for access to the Bodinnick vehicle ferry. The ferry has been moved from its old, steep and inconvenient slipway, which can still be seen beside the Riverside Hotel. Boat building yards, sail lofts and chandlers occupied the waterfront. Some remain but many of these premises are converted as holiday accommodation.

There always seems to be some activity in the harbour, but two spectacles in particular are the almost daily arrival and departure of clay ships – which also involve tug and pilot movements, and the regular evening races of Fowey's distinctive Troy class yachts – so named after the Fowey author Sir Arthur Quiller-Couch's novel *The Astonishing History of Troy Town* (a pseudonym for Fowey).

The clay wharves at Fowey

The Bodinnick Ferry c.1900

THE BODINNICK FERRY

The steep main street through Bodinnick descends to the slipway of the ancient Bodinnick Ferry, once part of the main route into south Cornwall, via the Cremyll Ferry at Plymouth. Evolving from a horseboat the ferry, has been maintained by two vehicle pontoons, manoeuvred by motor launches. Today a self propelled car and passenger pontoon, built in carries about 15 vehicles, running a shuttle service throughout the day. The old slip on the Fowey side can still be seen beside the Riverside Hotel.

The Bodinnick Ferry in 2002, pictured from the old ferry slip.

9

West Looe c1900

Truro in the 1950s with Coast Line's warehouse on the right

LOOE. An ancient port at the confluence of the East and West Looe rivers. Separated by the river, East Looe and West Looe were at one time separate boroughs. East Looe grew as the seaport for the Caradon mining district and quays now serving as car parks were once busy mineral quays, exporting copper ore and granite and importing coal for mine engines. The car park upstream of the road bridge occupies the site of a goods yard for the Liskeard and Looe Railway – which itself replaced the earlier six mile long Liskeard & Looe Union Canal of 1828.

A fishing fleet is still maintained on the quay in East Looe and a new fish market indicates a recent revival in its prosperity. The Banjo Pier extends from East Looe, forming a breakwater and offering protection south easterly gales.

Truro 1896

TRURO. Quays have existed at the confluence of the Rivers Kenwyn and Allen for over eight centuries. During the fourteenth century tin was smelted in works near the river's edge and shipped out from the Port of Truro's quays. Once the authority for almost the entire Fal Estuary, the port now extends only to the St Just and Mylor Pools in the Carrick Roadstead.

Only a small stretch of Lemon Quay – one of the earliest trading quays – survives. The majority of the quay and the River Kenwyn along which it stood, is covered over to form a car park. At the point of land formed by the confluence of Truro's two rivers is Town Quay. The large concrete building on the quay was built for Coast Lines Ltd (who maintained coastal passenger and goods services around the British Isles), and replaced an earlier warehouse. The Harbourmaster's office alongside dates back to the nineteenth century. Opposite Town Quay, adjoining the ring road, is Worth's Quay, a landing place for passenger boats from Falmouth since at least the 1870s. Backing onto Malpas Road are a range of river front warehouses. Immediately downstream of Town Quay is Garras Wharf, once the warehouses and timber ponds of Harveys timber merchants, but now totally redeveloped as a supermarket and car park.

The limited navigation available on the Truro River can be observed from Boscawen Park at low tide. The winding river channel is plainly discernable in the muddy estuary. Below Boscawen Park is Sunny Corner where Charles Dyer built wooden trading vessels on the banks of the river.

JOY! HEALTH! & PEACE
BE YOURS ON CHRISTMAS DAY

Town Quay, Falmouth. Vessels include the schooner MARY MILLER managed by C. W. Couch of Fowey, and the Kingsbridge built smack JNR of 1893. Fishing vessels include diesel engined former Mounts Bay pilchard drivers

FALMOUTH. In recent years Falmouth's waterfront has undergone much redevelopment, most of which are 'exclusive', both in terms of the purchasers they aim to attract and for the reduction of public access to the waterfront. Not long ago there were many steep and mysterious flights of steps, winding their way past warehouses and dwellings leading to the water's edge, inviting the inquisitive to explore. In common with many footpaths, public right of way to the water via these lanes and steps needed to be maintained, but little or no public outcry has been made about their wholesale loss.

Greenbank Quay remains at the northern end of the harbour. The beach alongside was used as a graving beach for the annual careening of harbour vessels. The waterfront from Greenbank

One of the last semi-accessible steps to Falmouth's waterfront.

Park to the Royal Cornwall Yacht Club, was once owned by the Olver family

Falmouth ship repair docks in 2002

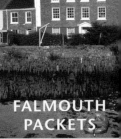

FALMOUTH PACKETS

Flushing waterfront

In 1688 Falmouth packets won the contract for the Iberian mail (to Corunna), followed later by contracts for Lisbon, West Indies, North America, Bermuda, Jamaica and Brazil. By 1827 some forty packets were based at Falmouth, engaged in the maintenance of Post Office mail contracts. The introduction of steam in the second quarter of the 1800s signaled their decline. By 1850 Liverpool, Plymouth and Southampton had replaced Falmouth as the main ports for foreign mails.

FLUSHING. The waterfront which survives today was largely developed during the seventeenth century by Samuel Trefusis. The dry stone construction of the quay walls have stood the test of time and are said to be the work of Dutch engineers. Adjacent to the watermen's shelter, at the back of Old Quay, is the last remaining wall of Samuel Trefusis' Great Cellars, a warehouse built for the Post Office Packets – many of the Captains of which lived in Flushing.

11

Laid-up shipping in the Fal in 1984 - a common feature in the King Harry and Tolverne reaches.

who maintained quays and warehouses for their building, contracting and general merchants trades. A number of building slips, quays and warehouses existed along Admiral's Quay up to the Prince of Wales Pier. Their haphazard development was characteristic of any busy nineteenth century waterfront. These quays suffered decline during the twentieth century, probably due more to chronic disrepair than lack of commercial use. Most of these buildings have gone, replaced by waterside apartments.

The foundation stone of the Prince of Wales Pier was laid by the Prince of Wales in 1903. Construction was completed in 1905. Post war modernisation has replaced the original Edwardian pier 'furniture' with the surviving concrete 'lido' style shelters and railings etc. Observation of the stonework at the landward end of the pier will reveal a number of different stone courses and building styles. The oldest part, near the pier approaches, are believed to date back to the seventeenth century.

Fish Strand Quay adjacent to the Prince of Wales Pier, served the nearby fish market and landed mail from the Post Office packets. The car park adjacent to the Fish Strand Quay was the site

of Falmouth's gasworks, where coal was discharged directly from colliers at the gasworks' own quay.

A series of quays, most of which are now built upon, back off Arwenack Street and extend all the way to the trio of North Quay, Customs House Quay and Town Quay. These three quays enclose the Inner Basin. Parts of North and Customs House Quays date from the seventeenth century. On Customs House Quay, running parallel to Arwenack Street, are the Harbourmaster's Office and Customs House (1814). At the entrance to Town Quay stands a whitewashed watermen's shelter. In Arwenack Street, opposite the access road to the basin, are the red brick offices of G. C. Fox, Shipping Agents, established here in 1790.

The area of land between the above mentioned quays and Falmouth Docks has been gradually infilled and redeveloped. This area, which sweeps around to The Bar, was once occupied by a tide pool and the slipways of steel shipbuilders: W. H. Lean; Charles Burt; Messrs Pool, Skinner & Williams; and Falmouth's premier steel ship builder, Cox & Co.

Below the headland of Pendennis lay the modern ship repair docks, founded in 1860. A good viewpoint of the docks and Falmouth Harbour can be obtained from the Castle Drive, directly above the docks. Free parking and coin operated telescopes are available.

The new National Maritime Museum Cornwall is nearing completion as this book goes to press. The impressive building is located near the docks.

On many evenings throughout the year, Falmouth's gaff cutter 'Working Boats' race. This class of sailing vessel has evolved from the sailing craft that have long dredged for oysters in the estuary (as the use of motor boats over the oyster beds is prohibited), and 'Quay Punts' – boats which raced out to meet incoming vessels and claim the right to tender for her whilst she was moored in the Carrick Roads.

The new National Maritime Museum Cornwall nearing completion in 2002.

PENRYN RIVER
FLUSHING QUAY (OLD QUAY)
FLUSHING
NEW QUAY
GREENBANK QUAY
KILN QUAY
TREFUSIS POINT
FALMOUTH HARBOUR CARRICK ROADS
PRINCE OF WALES PIER
FISH STRAND
WESTERN BREAKWATER
FALMOUTH DOCKS
NORTH QUAY
TOWN QUAY
EASTERN BREAKWATER
CUSTOMS HOUSE QUAY
DRY DOCKS
FALMOUTH
RAILWAY STATION
CASTLE DRIVE
PENDENNIS CASTLE
GYLLYNGVASE BEACH
FALMOUTH BAY
PENDENNIS POINT
SWANPOOL

South Quay, Penzance c1910

PENZANCE. An early Mounts Bay fishing harbour, Penzance was also a Coinage Town and tin exporter during the seventeenth century. The Old Pier was built in 1766 and extended in 1785 and 1812. The Albert Pier was completed in 1853. Other major harbour works of the nineteenth century included the construction of a floating harbour in 1884. A private dry dock was built by Nicholas Holman's foundry in 1880, to replace an older one. When a new road to the railway station was built along the harbour front, the Ross Swing Bridge was put in to enable vessels to enter the dry dock.

The Trinity House Depot was established at Penzance in 1866. It served lighthouses and navigational markers from Trevose to Start Point, including the Isles of Scilly. The main building along the harbour road – the Buoy Store – is now the National Lighthouse Centre.

Penzance has always been the mainland port for services to the Isles of Scilly. The 1,255 ton Scillonian III, built by Appledore Shipbuilders in 1977, currently maintains the daily passenger and cargo service to the islands and can usually be seen departing early in the morning and arriving back in the evening.

HAYLE. Between 1710 and 1720 two tin smelting houses were established in Hayle, importing coal from south Wales for the smelting process. Copper smelting was also undertaken – giving the name Copperhouse to a district to the east of the town. John Harvey established a foundry at the water's edge in 1779. A weir and floodgates were erected at the head of the creek, from where water was

released occasionally to help scour the navigable channel alongside Harvey's coal quays. Here the foundry company built a 450 yards long wharf in 1819. The opposing Copperhouse Company built their own Copperhouse Quay adjoining it. Harveys' foundry became the most important In Cornwall employing, at times, 1,000 men. The foundry manufactured mine engines and other mining equipment, but this declined after the 1860s with the closure of so many mines.

Having acquired their first small sloop in 1787 the Harveys' fleet gradually increased, with some ships adapted to moving large steam engine parts for delivery from the foundry. They could also import coal and pig iron, carried from south Wales in their own ships. In 1831 Harveys established a steam packet service to Bristol, which in 1841 linked with the Great Western Railway from London. It was barely surprising that Harveys began shipbuilding, and after the launch of the *John*

Trinity House National Lighthouse Centre, Penzance

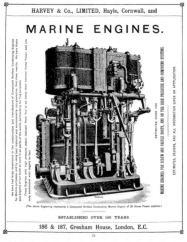

Advertisement for Harvey's marine engines.

Harvey in 1834, one or two new vessels were built and added to the fleet each year, mostly schooners up to about 70 feet in length. It was then an obvious move into iron shipbuilding, and some notable – and fast – paddle steamers were built for the Bristol Packet service. The most famous of these was the *Cornubia* of 1858, which was to be sold as a blockade runner for the Confederate States of America, during the American Civil War. The largest vessel built at Hayle was the *Ramleh*, launched in 1891, but falling prices and competition from the larger up-country shipyards ended this branch of the business, The Harveys' foundry itself closed in 1904.

The harbour entrance has never been easy, and dredging was required when sizable ships used the port. The electricity power station and small oil company depot were supplied by sea until the 1970s, and this formed the last regular cargoes.

PADSTOW. The tidal reaches of the River Camel provide the main estuarine haven on the northern coast of Cornwall. Located in the estuary is north Cornwall's largest port – Padstow. Padstow's first stone pier was built some time before 1536. In the sixteenth century the port engaged in trade with Wales, Ireland and ports in the Bristol Channel. During the seventeenth and eighteenth centuries slate, tin and copper ore were exported. The port became a Customs base to counter smuggling on this isolated stretch of coastline. Customs officers, Preventive men and Coastguards were responsible for the immediate north Cornwall coast. The original Customs House, together with a grain warehouse, are now converted as the Old Customs House Inn on South Quay. Emigrant ships for Canada left from Padstow during the nineteenth century, offering a new start to miners from the declining mining industry. In the early twentieth century the port was used by herring fleets, to get their fish to Billingsgate via the London & South Western Railway at Padstow – the fish sheds opposite the former railway station were also built by the railway company. China clay was exported, brought to the quayside from Wenford Bridge by the railway – the branch line closed in 1966.

Six shipbuilding yards once occupied Padstow's foreshore. In the 1800s these were located at St George's Well (downstream from Padstow), Lower Yard (now North Quay waterside flats), North Jetty, South Quay, Higher Yard (near the fish shed site) and Dennis Cove (where ships of 800 tons were built). During this period the port became active in ship management

Padstow Harbour c1900

Padstow's floating harbour.

BOSCASTLE

BOSCASTLE. A spectacular twisting entrance to this picturesque cove has rendered Boscastle a favourite of visitors to the north Cornwall coast. Despite commercialism at the landward end of the village, the waterfrontage along the harbour remains unspoilt, thanks largely to its ownership by the National Trust.

Boscastle's first pier was erected in the sixteenth century to protect the inner cove from the action of the sea. This pier was soon destroyed, but later in the century a second one was built and it is largely this structure which stands on the southern shore. In 1740 it was extensively restored.

A fleet of trading vessels was maintained by the port, exporting manganese ore from mines near Launceston during the early nineteenth century, and china clay from Bodmin Moor later in the century. Other exports included slate, corn and bark.

A second breakwater projects into the narrow entrance from the northern shore, to help break the seas which rush into the ravine. However, in the event of bad weather trading vessels left the quayside and took the ground of the harbour, held down by strong hawsers. These especially thick ropes were kept at Boscastle and made available by the Harbourmaster

and deep sea trading, and Padstow was for time a shipowning community. In 1823 there were 27 registered shipowning ventures in the town.

The sand banks at the estuary mouth, and in particular the notorious Doom Bar, have restricted Padstow's growth as a major sea port. In 1829 the Padstow Harbour Association set up capstans on Stepper Point, at the mouth of the estuary, to improve navigation into the port by warping ships into the estuary against the elements.

Owing to the dangerous coast and estuary mouth a lifeboat was established before 1825. In 1856 the RNLI assumed control of the station at Hawkers Cove, inside the mouth of the estuary. In 1967 the lifeboat station was moved to Mother Ivey's Bay on Trevose Head. A Land Rover, based in Padstow, takes the crew to the lifeboat some three miles distant. A new Tyne class lifeboat was delivered in 1984.

Today a small fishing fleet is maintained. A controversial flood prevention and sewage-scheme development has resulted in the old inner harbour becoming a floating harbour and yacht basin.

The Rock Ferry which crosses the estuary from the ferry steps at the end of North or Ferry Jetty, is run by the Harbour Commissioners. This jetty was built in 1931 by a labour force drawn from the unemployed.

Boscastle

SIENE BOAT MARKINGS

BOLITHO

J. TREMEARNE

C. TREMEARNE

ROSS & CO

J. QUICK

T. JENKYN

SHORT & DUNN

FISHING

Foremost in the calendar of many Cornish fishing villages was the pilchard season which began around July and lasted for about four months. This modestly sized, oily fish, the adult of the sardine, was responsible for the development of virtually all of Cornwall's picturesque coastal fishing villages and coves. Until these communities were 'discovered' by nineteenth and twentieth century visitors their economic survival depended on the pilchard.

Smoked, pickled or (exclusively by the nineteenth century) salted, pilchards found an inexhaustible market in Mediterranean countries, particularly during the Lenten fasts of Catholics. Pilchards numbering in millions raced towards the Cornish coast each year. Huge shoals darkened the water and obligingly divided at Lands End to feed Sennen, St Ives and the northern coast, while the southern shoals were gathered in Mounts Bay, off the Lizard, Falmouth Bay, St Austell Bay, Looe and Cawsand Bay. This pilchard fishery remained an almost entirely Cornish phenomenon.

SEINE FISHING

Complete shoals of pilchards numbering at times 200 hogsheads (2,500 to 3,000 pilchards per hogshead – i.e. half a million) were taken in a day. Shoals were encircled by seine nets, hauled into shallow 'shoal' water and anchored. Pilchard seining was undertaken by seine companies with names such as the Unity Seine and the Bolitho Western Seine. Each seine usually had three boats, two nets and fish cellars, or 'palaces', ashore, The first boat was the low and broad seine boat, up to 40 feet, in length. It was six oared, crewed by seven or eight men and carried the seine net which was shot around the shoal. The second boat was the follower, variously corrupted around the coast as follier, vollier or volyer, which carried the stop or tuck net, used to lift the fish from the water. Pilchards were then transferred to gurries (barrows) or maunds (baskets) in which they were carried ashore to the bulking house. The third boat was the lurker, lurcher or larker, a smaller, faster boat of four oars which carried the Master Seiner, who directed the operation. A cliff top look out 'huer' sometimes directed the seines with semaphore signals.

At St Ives there was room for 20 seines to be worked at any one time. By 1870 there were over 280 seine companies registered in this port alone. Each seine was allocated a 'stem' to work, while signals on Porthminster Beach notified change over times.

Shovelling pilchards into carts at Sennen Cove

Lifting pilchards from the seine net with tuck baskets

ST IVES. St Ives' first stone pier was built for the protection of fishing vessels during the fifteenth century. An outer pier was designed by John Smeaton, and was completed in 1770. This pier was extended between 1888 and 1890, but the original section remains, marked by the circular structure in the centre which used to be the lighthouse at what was the end of the pier. Between 1864 and 1867 an outer wooden pier was erected to help enclose the beach. This structure suffered from storm damage and only a short stone stump at the landward end now remains. The West Pier was built in 1894 for shipping roadstone from local quarries.

Tin and copper from the St Just district was exported from St Ives and the port had long attracted a general cargo trade. But St Ives was primarily a fishing port, supporting both drift and seine fisheries. As the principal pilchard fishery in Cornwall, St Ives became so busy that Acts of Parliament were necessary in 1776 and 1811 to regulate the fishery. The fishing trade peaked in the 1830s and '40s with the port catching an average 22 million pilchards per year. Huers were stationed at Carn Crowse, Porthminster Point and Carrack Gladden Point, both to direct the seines and to signal change over times of seines working allotted stems. In 1905 there were still 200 fishing vessels registered, but the trade was in decline. Seining was nearly over by 1914, although seines were registered until 1920 The harbour is filled with pleasure craft today, but not entirely to the exclusion of fishing. St Ives' art colony has made good use of the old shore facilities. Along the top of Porthmeor Beach is a row of sail lofts that have long been converted to artists studios, while the Penwith Galleries in St Ives are converted pilchard cellars.

Contrary to the name of one siening venture – the Poor Man's Adventure Seine, seining was a rich mans fishery – during the nineteenth century each company required about £1,000 capital to establish – to buy the boats, nets and shore facilities, and to pay the fishermen and shore based workers. Although the season only lasted a few months, with good fortune, investors could recoup their capital in their first year.

Once ashore in the curing cellars or palaces, the pilchards were bulked or balked – salted in layers, packed heads out and tails towards the centre. The resulting pilchard oil which drained off was sold separately. Fishing families salted about 1,500 to 2,000 fish for their own consumption during the winter.

Porthmeor Beach, St Ives.
The old net and sail lofts are now artists' studios.

ST. IVES HARBOUR, BAITING LINES

St Ives with siene boats and drifters

ASHORE. Large numbers were employed in St Ives, Newlyn and the other pilchard fisheries gutting, salting and packing the fish. The oil of the pilchard was used in oil lamps. Murray's Handbook for Travellers in 1851 suggested that 'St Ives though highly picturesque (is) most abominably tainted with the effluvia of the fish cellars'. The huge nets, large enough to surround a shoal, had to be made and maintained, and tanned to preserve the natural fibres of which they were made. The export of pilchards to the Mediterranean called for vast supplies of casks, and so every fishing village needed coopers to make these and timber staves were imported to make them, while the village blacksmith would

By 1870 there were 379 seines in Cornwall located as follows:	
St.Ives	285
Mounts Bay	23
Mevagissey	10
Newquay	9
St Mawes	9
others	43

make the iron bands to seal them tightly together.

The fishing boats and larger wooden ships had to be carefully looked after if they were to remain seaworthy. Timber ships were preserved with natural tar, pitch and bitumen, their joints caulked with oakum and pitch which required regular attention. The rigging of hemp rope required regular treatment and sails of flax canvas were waxed or tanned. All this gave jobs to men on shore in the boat repair yards, or employment to the fishermen when the season or the weather stopped them going to sea. A glance in Kelly's Directory of Cornwall – the Victorian equivalent of our Yellow Pages – gives some idea of this landbound side of maritime life. As late as 1897 entries included: 20 Sailmakers, 14 Shipbuilders, 24 Ship's Chandlers, 68 Pilots, 20 Rope and Twine makers and 1 Ships pump maker. At the same time no less than 261 Master Mariners were listed.

Fish packing at St Ives

DRIFTFISHING

Towards the end of the nineteenth century the pilchard shoals inexplicably began to desert the Cornish coast. Already by the 1850s Cornwall's drift fishery had gained the ascendancy over the seine fishery.

Before the seventeenth century drift nets had been used to catch pilchards and other fish

Mending nets at St Ives

further offshore. A long standing feud developed, the seiners claiming that the driving boats were breaking up the shoals before the seines could enclose them. The Long Parliament of the Restoration restricted the use of drift nets to three miles offshore from June to November inclusive.

Whilst ownership of a seine company represented a considerable investment, a driving boat, with nets, cost around £250 in the early nineteenth century – still a big investment – but, in partnership with others, attainable for the fishermen themselves. Builders like William Paynter of St Ives, Blewett of Newlyn, James Wills of Penzance and Bowden and Kitto of Porthleven, built pilchard drivers – lug sailed, half decked, about 28 feet long; and mackerel drivers – two masted luggers, fully decked and up to 50 feet in length. Luggers built in south east Cornwall, from Mevagissey to Looe, had square transoms. St Ives, Penzance and Newlyn boats had a sharp stem to save space in crowded harbours. Those of Porthleven had a rounded counter stern to give protection from the following seas encountered on the east side of Mounts Bay. St Ives boats had rounder bilges, to take the

ground in the drying harbour. Mounts Bay boats, inside their better protected harbours used wooden legs when lying on the beach. At Polperro a smaller boat was developed, gaff rigged but without a boom. At Mevagissey similar small boats were called Toshers.

The mackerel season lasted from January to

Lug sailed drift boats at Looe. FY 233 Guide Me (below right) is pictured on the right in 1993 (Courtesy Julie Brickhill), While Guiding Star FY363 (below middle and page 2) also survives as gaff rigged ketch.

June. The drift fleet worked off the Eddystone and the Isles of Scilly, sailing out into the Atlantic west of Wolf Rock during the main season. From June to August herring were fished in the Irish and North Seas followed by the pilchard season and handlining for hake – which followed the pilchard shoals.

In addition to the seine and drift fleets, crabbing boats around the entire coast set pots offshore. The Sennen Cove crabber, a two masted, lug sailed boat, about 20 feet long, was one example of a fishing craft developed locally to suit the environment of the particular harbour or cove. At Saltash on the Tamar, in the Carrick Roadstead and on the Helford River, oyster beds were dredged. The Falmouth working boat, a smack rigged gaffer, was developed to work the oyster beds. A few examples of wooden hulled working boats survive, one of the oldest being the yellow hulled *Victory*. Moulds have been taken off these vessels to produce a growing number of glass fibre versions which race regularly in the Carrick Roads.

Once Cornwall's railways were linked to the mainline from London in 1859, the railway opened up new, larger markets. 'Foreign' fleets were attracted to the Cornish fishing grounds, including trawlers from Plymouth, Brixham and the East Coast. Penzance became the main Cornish harbour for the East Coast fleet.

The drift fleet fell into decline during the early twentieth century. In 1920 the last pilchard driver was fitted out with engines at Newlyn, just one example of a Cornish driving boat has survived, the

In 1870 there were 645 driving boats registered in Cornwall:	
Newlyn	130
Mousehole	105
Porthleven	104
St. Ives	186
Mevagissey	61
Looe	22
others, in 7 other ports	37

Newlyn, looking across from the original pier

Barnabas, a mackerel driver, built in St Ives in 1881 is maintained in sailing condition by the Cornish Friends of the Maritime Trust.

Fishing remains an important Cornish industry, as can be seen by the extensive improvements which have been made in Newlyn with a new and often crowded jetty. The industry has changed out of all recognition in recent years; foreign factory-ships are to be seen off-shore, and with modern technological developments extensive over-fishing of many species has resulted. Regulations are imposed with political directives and controls from Whitehall and Brussels. Many see this bureaucratic interference as a present day phenomenon, but the truth is that fisheries in Cornwall have been subject to tythes, taxes and strict control for as long as records exist.

MEVAGISSEY. In contrast to the nearby clay ports of St Austell Bay, Mevagissey's history dates back centuries to medieval times and owes its existence, not to the wealth of the land but to fishing, in particular pilchard seining.

The first stone built, protecting pier was built during the fifteenth century. In 1775 an Act was obtained to build a pier enclosing the present day inner harbour. Exposed to south easterly gales the pier suffered continual damage, so two outer piers were built, creating an outer harbour, which was completed in 1897 – commemorated by a plaque in the South Pier parapet.

In the early nineteenth century there were 30 pilchard seines registered in the harbour and by 1850 Mevagissey supported some 80 fishing vessels – increasingly lug sailed drifters, as the drift fishery supplanted the seines. These Cornish luggers measured about 40 feet, and Mevagissey also developed its own, distinctive, 20 ft longliner fishing boats, known as Toshers. The builders of these boats included Henry Roberts, Willie Frasier and, well into twentieth century, Percy Mitchell at nearby Pormellon. Today John Moores shipyard still builds boats on Frasier's old site, near the Museum. Longliner fishing continues today, the boats can usually be seen in St Austell Bay, but the catch is generally taken to the fish markets of Newlyn or Looe.

Mevagissey Museum is well worth a visit and is packed with maritime memorabilia.

The inner harbour, Mevagissey

FISHING REGISTRY

The change of port authorities can be noted by the registration port initials painted on the fishing boats:

PW – Padstow

SS – St Ives

PZ – Penzance

FH – Falmouth

FY – Fowey

PH – Plymouth
(Tamar to Seaton Bay)

21

Gaff rigged long liners at Polperro - similar boats were developed in Mevagissey

PORTLOE. A particularly attractive fishing village set amid spectacular cliff scenery. Portloe once supported a small drift fleet and a seine fishery. The natural harbour has no jetties, so trading ketches landed on the beach. Notable near the harbour mouth is the extremely steep lifeboat slipway. The lifeboat house survives, converted for domestic use. Sufficient fishing and lobster potting continues to provide Portloe with an authentic air.

ST MAWES. St Mawes is a beautifully located fishing village which once maintained pilchard, crabbing and oyster fisheries. St Mawes' first stone per was built in 1536 and the St Mawes Pier & Harbour Company improved the pier and harbour in 1854. Some Falmouth Harbour pilots were also based here, the location proving more suitable than Falmouth, both for seeing incoming ships and getting out to sea aboard their pilot cutters.

The Peters family's small boatyard, begun in 1790, was famous for the fast six oared pilot gigs; the racing of these gigs, which takes place in the summer, has once again become popular and now more gigs are being built to the same pattern that Peters was using in the early 1800s. St Mawes today appears picturesque, but little remains of the original fishing village or the local atmosphere.

St Mawes

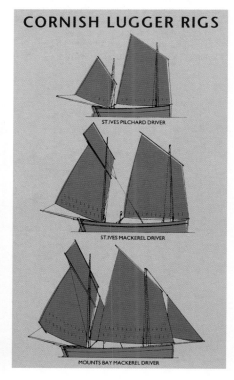

CORNISH LUGGER RIGS

ST.IVES PILCHARD DRIVER

ST.IVES MACKEREL DRIVER

MOUNTS BAY MACKEREL DRIVER

Polpeor Cove - the southernmost point of England

Porthleven

PORTHOUSTOCK. A fishing cove dominated by the loading jetties of the adjacent roadstone quarries. It was to these Lizard quarries that river barges of the Fal estuary came, loading roadstone under the chutes and taking it to Tresillian Quay. The chutes went out of use in 1958. There was a similar system in use at nearby Dean Quarry. Porthoustock was a lifeboat station from 1869 to 1945. In the churchyard of St Keverne, above Porthoustock, is the Mohegan Memorial which commemorates the wreck of that liner on the Manacle Rocks off Porthoustock in 1898, with the loss of 106 lives.

COVERACK. A pilchard fishing and crab potting village, the small harbour is built of the local serpentine stone, with an inscribed stone dated 1724.

CADGWITH. Pilchard seining, crab potting and smuggling have all thrived here. A lifeboat arrived in 1867, and the station was active for almost a century until amalgamated with the Lizard station in 1961 – with the opening of the new Lizard station at Kilcobben Cove

CHURCH COVE (LANDEWEDNACK). The pilchard cellars building remains. There is also a boat winch at the top of the extremely steep slipway. The surviving lifeboat house was for the reserve Lizard boat, launched from here if weather conditions were unsuitable in Polpeor Cove. The station closed in 1899 after just two service launches.

POLPEOR COVE. The most southerly point on the British mainland. The cove saw some beach trading and the Lizard Lifeboat was stationed here from 1859 to 1960.

MULLION COVE. A fishing village with a protective pier which supported pilchard seines but at there were no curing cellars in the village, the fish were taken to Newlyn. There was a lifeboat here from 1867 to 1908.

PORTHLEVEN. A fishing village prior to the building of the present harbour. which was completed in 1818. These works, on the exposed south-west facing coast of Mount's Bay were destroyed in a storm in 1824 and subsequently rebuilt. The promoters of the development sought general and mining trade – coal and timber in, minerals out. The harbour did not prove satisfactory and the venture failed. The company was bought out by Harvey's of Hayle in 1855. Harveys improved the harbour, building the long breakwater to protect the entrance and trade increased. But despite this phase Porthleven has continued much as it did before, as a fishing and boatbuilding harbour, with a useful inner basin, the legacy of Harveys' unfulfilled plans.

Cadgwith

Sennen Cove

NEWLYN. Newlyn was a medieval fishery and its original fifteenth century pier survives within the subsequently enlarged harbour. During the eighteenth and nineteenth centuries Newlyn expanded as a major fishery with pilchard seines, mackerel and herring fisheries and the most important drift fleet in Cornwall. Between 1866 and 1873 the harbour and quays were extended. The North or Victoria Pier was built in 1888. Newlyn remains as Cornwall's major fishing port, under the management of the Newlyn Pier and Harbour Commissioners. A major expansion of fishing facilities, with a new pier built into the centre of the harbour, was completed in the 1980s. These facilities are used not only by its own fleet, out also by trawlers from the east coast and the continent, although without the problems that arose in the past with the arrival, of 'foreign' fishermen. In the Newlyn Riots of 1896 fighting broke out when east coast fishermen went to sea on a Sunday which could not be tolerated by the strict Methodist fishermen of the village.

For many years the South Pier has been reserved for the roadstone quarries at nearby Penlee Point; formerly the stone was transported onto the quay by a narrow gauge railway from the quarry.

MOUSEHOLE. An ancient fishing harbour which supported pilchard and mackerel fishing. Mousehole was the first harbour in the county to have a pier, which was built during the last decade of the fourteenth century, when it was the most important fishing place in Cornwall. In 1849 over 800 people, including packers, curers and coopers were employed in the harbour's fishing trade – 425 being fishermen.

The ancient pier was extended in 1840 and again in 1861 when a new pier was built. At the harbour entrance, as protection in heavy weather, baulks of timber may be placed between the piers, to stop the sea breaking into the harbour. Until the 1970s a timber crane stood on the south side of the entrance to handle these considerable baulks.

PENBERTH. As at other small coves in Penwith, a narrow and steep beach has been used for fishing over the centuries, but beaching boats must always have been a problem. Here, as at Porthgwarra, a large windlass or capstan was used to haul boats up above high tide level, but the example at Penberth has survived and been restored, thanks to the National Trust, who own the cove.

SENNEN COVE. In 1850 there were 18 fishing vessels registered in Sennen, employing some 80 people. Pilchards represented the major catch, but the cove was also frequented by shoals of red mullet. the Round House as Sennen housed a capstan for pulling the boats up onto the beach. The pier was built in 1908 to offer protection to shipping and the lifeboat. Sennen has been a lifeboat station since 1853. This most westerly village in mainland England still maintains crab and lobster potting.

PORT QUIN. One of the three porths centred around Port Isaac, Port Quin was a small fishing village. Pilchard seines and shellfish pots were maintained. A limited beach trade brought in coal and manure – agricultural work being an alternative occupation for the villagers. The fish cellars still stand, but together with the stores and other cottages, have been converted for holiday accommodation.

Owned today by the National Trust, Port Quin is notable as a dead or deserted village. A degree of mystery surrounds its demise. Unfortunately, surviving records of the village lend themselves to differing interpretations. It can only be said, with any certainty, that the fishing fleet ceased to exist near the end of the nineteenth century and the population dwindled rapidly.

Port Quin

Smuggling in Cornwall has been romanticised by a succession of novelists and, perhaps most extremely, by the county's tourist trade – whimsical Treasure Island-like characters adorn café signs, amusement arcades and tourist attractions. The truth about this illegal activity however is probably stranger than the fiction.

Smuggling became an economic necessity for many in Cornwall, particularly after a Salt Duty was imposed during the late seventeenth century (salt from the continent was used for curing pilchards). This was one of the mainstays of the Cornish fishing industry and a major source of winter food throughout the county. The duty sometimes could amount to about half of the fishermens' meagre income. Therefore salt was smuggled in to avoid paying the tax. It is probably more correct to say that salt was imported into isolated fishing villages and coves as before, but the cargoes remained undeclared to the authorities. However, the opportunity was also taken to trade in other heavily taxed, less essential commodities such as brandy, tea and tobacco. The higher the import tariffs were raised, the more lucrative became the profit for smugglers. This activity, known as 'free trading', was supported by a sympathetic local population, and many members of the local community, including the local gentry – who had tythes, leases and investments to protect – often colluded in the trade.

In Polperro, Zephania Job was entrusted by the free traders with their finances; Job meticulously maintained their accounts and himself backed various smuggling ventures, later establishing his own note-issuing bank. Capt James Dunn of Mevagissey was a wealthy master mariner, shipbuilder, shipowner and smuggler – reputedly Mevagissey was largely rebuilt from the proceeds of the free trade. Sir John Knill served as Mayor of St Ives and was the Collector of Customs for the area (the top man). He also, reputedly, backed many of the smuggling ventures in the district.

Merchants in Guernsey specialised in supplying goods to the Cornish free traders. One of the most powerful suppliers was Carteret Priaulx & Co., once the largest commercial trading house in Guernsey. The company's agents toured Cornwall to tout for business. Government observers recorded cargoes and ships names at the quayside in Guernsey, but could only gain a smuggling conviction if they were caught in the act of landing goods illegally. Customs officials had few resources at their disposal and received little or no assistance from the local population. In Fowey, in 1835, five men charged with being amongst some 100 smugglers who had fought Preventive men were acquitted after Crown jury decided that the sticks with which they had been armed were not offensive weapons.

Favoured destinations for landing smuggled goods included Mounts Bay, the Fal Estuary, Portloe and Looe, but Cawsand, Polperro and Mevagissey remained the chief strongholds of the free trade.

Eight oared volyer boats from the pilchard seines were favoured for landing goods. The principal cross channel smuggling craft were cutters and sloops, which were fast and could easily be beached in secluded coves. The free traders' boats were invariably faster than the Government craft, while the smugglers possessed an intimate knowledge of their local waters. In the 1770s it was estimated that some 469,000 gallons of brandy and 350,000 pounds of tea were being smuggled into the country annually.

Sloop rig c1800, favoured by free traders

continued on page 28

Padstow No 2 Lifeboat

LIFEBOATS

Looe Lifeboat 1866-1930 East Looe. 1992- Inshore Lifeboat, East Looe
Fowey Lifeboat 1859-1922 Polkerris. 1922- at Albert Quay, Fowey (took over from Polkerris). 1995 Inshore Lifeboat.
Mevagissey Lifeboat 1869-1888 at Portmellon. 1888-1930 Mevagissey Harbour.
Portloe Lifeboat 1870-1887.
Falmouth Lifeboat 1867- southern end of Falmouth Harbour. 1980 - Inshore Lifeboat
Porthoustock Lifeboat 1869-1942.
Coverack Lifeboat 1901-1972. Inshore Lifeboat withdrawn 1978.
Cadgwith Lifeboat 1867-1963.
The Lizard Lifeboat 1859-1961 Polpeor Cove. 1885-1899 Church Cove (No 2 Lizard Lifeboat station). 1961- Kilcobben Cove.
Mullion Lifeboat 1867-1908
Porthleven Lifeboat 1863-1929.
Marazion Lifeboat 1990- Inshore Lifeboat
Penzance Lifeboat 1803-1917 Penzance Harbour. 1908-1913 Newlyn Harbour. 1913- 1983 Penlee Point. 1983- Newlyn Harbour.
Sennen Cove Lifeboat 1853- extant. 1994- Inshore Lifeboat
St Ives Lifeboat 1840- extant. 1964- Inshore Lifeboat
Hayle Lifeboat 1866-1920
St Agnes 1968 - Inshore Lifeboat
Newquay Lifeboat 1860 - 1945. 1965 - Inshore Lifeboat.
Padstow Lifeboat 1827 - (since 1967 at Trevose Head).
Rock 1994 - Inshore Lifeboat
Port Issac Lifeboat 1869 - 1933. 1967- Inshore Lifeboat.
Bude Lifeboat 1853 - 1922. 1966 - Inshore Lifeboat.

Despite instances of long working lives for some ships an fishing boats, many did not survive but came to a dramatic end o the rocky Cornish coast or were simply overcome by storms out a sea. Seafaring and fishing were always hard and dangerou occupations, especially in the days of sail. The annals of th numerous lifeboat stations on the Cornish coast record acts o amazing bravery. Members of the maritime community would g off in any weather to man the lifeboats, many hundreds of live being saved over the years. Increasing maritime trade, especiall during the nineteenth century, added larger ships to the growin number of casualties along the dangerous Cornish coast - over thousand wrecks are documented around Cornwall and the Isles o Scilly. Sailing ships became embayed (i.e. unable to find sea roon to sail away from the shore, while tide and/or wind drove ther towards it). Steamships hit rocks through mistaken navigation. An today – with radar and satellite navigation promoting over confidence, even arrogance – ships and pleasure craft continue t come to grief along the Cornish shore. To help prevent thes accidents Trinity House has established a chain of coasta lighthouses around Cornwall, supplemented by fog signals lightships, buoys, daymarks and harbour lights. The Royal Nationa Lifeboat Institution meanwhile, has maintained a series of lifeboa stations around the coast. Both lightouses and lifeboats are an

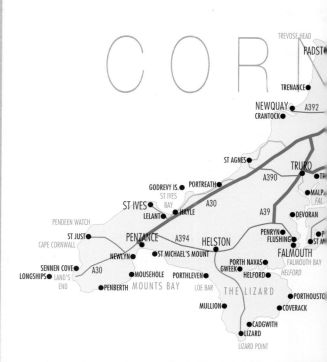

ntegral part of Cornwall's maritime heritage and their story is told
more completely in: *Cornwall's Lighthouse Heritage* by Michael
Tarrant, and *Cornwall's Lifeboat Heritage* by Nicholas Leach.

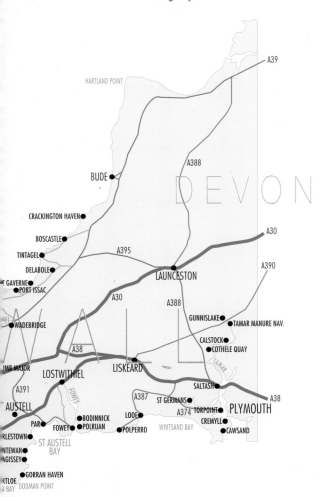

MARITIME LOCATIONS
IN CORNWALL

Pendeen Lighthouse

LIGHTHOUSES

Trevose Head Lighthouse 1847.
1 white flash every 7.5 seconds,
Godrevy Lighthouse 1859.
Flashing white/red every 10 seconds (red
only visible in danger sector)
Pendeen Lighthouse 1900.
4 white flashes every 15 seconds. Open
to the public by the Trevithick Trust.
Longships Lighthouse first 1795,
second 1873. Isophase (i.e. long flash
and equal period of darkness) every 10
seconds - white seaward, red landward.
Wolf Rock Lighthouse 1870.
1 white flash every 10 seconds.
Tater Du Lighthouse 1965.
3 white flashes every 15 seconds.
Lizard Lighthouse first established
1619. Present two towers built in 1752.
Eastern tower only 1 white flash every 3
seconds. Open to the public by the
Trevithick Trust.
St Anthony's Head Lighthouse 1835.
White isophase 15 seconds (with red only
visible in danger sector).
Eddystone Lighthouse First 1698.
Fourth 1759 - now on Plymouth Hoe.
Fifth and current 1882. Two white flashes
every 10 seconds (with fixed red only
visible in danger sector).

Smeaton's Eddystone Lighthouse of 1759

SMUGGLING (continued)

During the latter half of the eighteenth century the Government began to take steps to redress the balance. An anti smuggling Act of 1779 declared that ships under 200 tons, carrying illegal packages, would be forfeit. Between 1786 and 1815, 81 Fowey vessels were seized. Following a later Act, cutters were forfeit as smuggling craft unless they were square rigged, (fore and aft rigged vessels could sail very close to the wind outrunning larger, but square rigged government ships) or if they were fitted with a bowsprit larger than two thirds of the boat's length. Unless square rigged, or a sloop with a standing bowsprit, no vessel of any kind was to be clinker built. But such craft were still built and subsequently seized. In 1784 fast, long sailing ships, with a length more than $3^1/_2$ times their breadth, were banned unless licenced. Despite all these regulations, many 'illegal' vessels continued to be built, especially in Mevagissey and Fowey and, surprisingly, were even entered into the official Port register.

Some 29 vessels at this time were known by the authorities to be engaged in smuggling, but unlike free traders in the south east, most of the Cornishmen were armed. Around 300 seamen were engaged in the trade in Cornwall, backed up by a far larger number of landsmen. In 1809 the Preventive Water Guard was formed, equipped with galleys and gigs. They not only

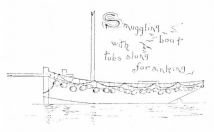

Contraband strung along the hull of the smuggler's boat ready for sinking in an emergency or in shoal water, for retrieval later.

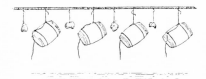

Contraband, weighted and ready for sinking.

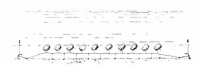

A contraband crop on the sea floor, awaiting collection

patrolled inshore along the free trader's coast, but additionally checked on the activity of the Revenue cutters further offshore. In 1816 the Revenue cutters were transferred to the jurisdiction of the Royal Navy. Ashore, Riding Officers patrolled the coast, with powers of search up to 10 miles inland. Violent clashes occurred, so an 'outside' armed and mounted force, the Inniskillen Dragoons, were billeted in Truro. In 1822 the Preventive Water Guard, Revenue cutters and Riding Officers were amalgamated to form the Coastguard. After 1841 the Customs House staff in the Port of Fowey – with jurisdiction over Mevagissey and Polperro – included: a Surveyor, Controller, Collector, three Officers, a Land Waiter (to keep watch over vessels in the harbour whereas a Tide Waiter could board a ship before it had anchored), three Salt Officers, a Searcher of Salt, and an Excise Officer. In addition, the Customs House received frequent calls from Riding Officers and cutters of the Coastguard.

An Act of 1805 extended the law against smuggling to 100 leagues from the mainland, the new area deliberately included the Channel Islands. No sooner was a Customs House established on the islands, than the French port of Roscoff was declared a free port to win the trade. But reductions in taxes, coupled with increased law enforcement, began to render the trade less attractive. By 1815 the 'acceptable' face of the old free trade was fading. Although old habits died slowly, particularly in south east Cornwall, smuggling or free trading had ceased to pose a significant problem by the second half of the nineteenth century.

CAWSAND & KINGSAND. Until 1854 Kingsand lay within the county of Devon, the stream behind the Halfway House Inn and a mark on the wall of a house in Garret Street serves to indicate the old boundary. The villages of Cawsand and Kingsand supported a fleet of small fishing smacks – or 'hookers', and pilchard seines. Some pilot boats for the Port of Plymouth were also based here. Cawsand Bay has long offered a sheltered anchorage from all except south easterly gales. In the last century the bay offered anchorage to some of the most renowned trans-Atlantic and other liners of the day, calling in at Plymouth to disembark passengers and mail.

Polperro

The proximity of these villages to the Three Towns of Plymouth, Devonport and Stonehouse, rendered it profitable as a base for smuggling. Contraband was landed, hidden and taken across the Tamar to the Three Towns in smaller quantities.

In his book, *Cornwall's Forgotten Corner*, Tony Carne recalls their house at the bottom of Garret Street, where his father uncovered a tunnel entrance in the cellar which came out in a cupboard of a house in St Andrew Street.

A row of Coastguard cottages were built in the 1820s, overlooking the beaches at Cawsand and Kingsand. But smuggling continued until declining economic returns and increased odds of being caught gradually made the risks less worthwhile Nevertheless, as late as 1870 Tony Carne's grandmother was occasionally used as a convincing decoy to a skin of brandy which was disguised as a baby in a pram. A boat was taken over to the notorious watermens' community of Mutton Cove in Devonport.

POLPERRO. Polperro supported seining and drift fishing. Its inner drying tidal harbour is protected by double piers with a narrow entrance, which could be protected by lowering timber baulks into slots at the end of each pier – since replaced by hydraulic rams. Alongside Mevagissey and Cawsand, Polperro ranks amongst the top three smuggling bases, where luggers for use by smugglers were built. Tom Potter of Polperro was hanged for killing Humphrey Glinn – a Revenue

Coastguard cottages overlooking Cawsand (seen through the trees on the right) were built to curb smuggling in the bay.

Prussia Cove

man trying to seize the smuggling lugger *Lottery*. Zephania Job, a school teacher in Polperro, was entrusted by the smuggling community to look after their finances, eventually acting as their agent, fixing deals with merchants in France and the Channel Islands. So successful was trade that Job established his own bank.

MEVAGISSEY. Thomas Shepherd of Mevagissey was a boatbuilder in the eighteenth century,

The Kings Pipe, Falmouth Customs House – for burning contraband tobacco.

famed for his fast craft which he built both for the 'Free Traders' and the Revenue. Capt James Dunn, a local shipbuilder and shipowner, was one of Mevagissey's principal smugglers during the late eighteenth century.

PRUSSIA COVE. This small cove between Helston and Penzance has been immortalised through *An Autobiography of a Cornish Smuggler*, based on the exploits of the Carter family. John Carter, known as the 'King of Prussia', and his brother Harry (a staunch Methodist), were local smugglers towards the end of the eighteenth century. The brothers were scrupulously honest with everybody except the Customs service – when the Revenue men seized one of their cargoes, John Carter broke into Penzance Custom House, apparently only recovering his own impounded property – not stealing others. Harry Carter commanded a succession of smuggling vessels, typically 50 to 60 tons and armed with sixteen guns. At one time, during the American War, when a Revenue cutter came close to the shore, John Carter, who had fortified the cove, fired on it using his shore battery. It was the Carters who christened Porth Lea as King's Cove or Prussia Cove, because in childhood games John Carter always adopted the identity of the 'King of Prussia'. One of the last of the smuggling Carter clan died in 1822, in nearby Breage – a village with notorious associations with the alleged activities of wreckers along the coast.

The legend lives on at Town Quay, Fowey

Granite and former mineral quays at Calstock on the River Tamar.

Just as Cornwall's fishing heritage is evidenced today by the existence of numerous coastal harbours, so too can the county's mining and quarrying industries be witnessed by dozens of ruined mine engine houses, spoil tips and man made craters. Cornwall was particularly well endowed with the largest deposits of tin and copper ore in Europe. Tin ore had been excavated in the county since prehistoric times and by the nineteenth century Cornwall was the most important source of copper ore in the world. Cornish granite quarries provided the raw materials for prestigious engineering works including the building of the Chelsea Embankment, London Bridge, Dover Harbour Improvements, Portland Naval Base and two consecutive Eddystone Lighthouses. Blue elvan roadstones and various granite chippings were won both from inland quarries and from spectacular cliff sites around the coast, while in north Cornwall a vast crater continues to offer up Delabole slate. Since the beginning of the last century, china clay has increased in importance, the majority coming from the area around St Austell.

It has been calculated that during the last century about 20,000,000 tons of copper ore, tin and china clay went away from Cornish ports, a not inconsiderable quantity, when it is remembered that most of this was carried on sailing ships with a capacity of 100 or 200 tons. Of this quantity, until about 1860, copper predominated, this being sent away as ore for smelting in south Wales, mostly in the Swansea valley. Returning ships carried coal which the deepening mines required for their steam pumping engines. As copper declined in the last decades of the century, so china clay increased in production to replace the metals as major cargoes. All of these minerals and stones were exported by sea from docks, jetties and beaches, bound in the main for British and continental ports. The earliest trade in tin to the Mediterranean certainly dates back 2000 years.

Tin and copper ore, granite and slate were laboriously transported to the nearest navigable point by packhorse. Such quays and landing places as were available were primarily fishing harbours: Boscastle with slate and mineral ores from Bodmin Moor; St Ives and Penzance with tin and copper from Penwith; and Looe, exporting tin and copper and granite from Caradon. Long established river landings included Padstow and Wadebridge on the River Camel with minerals and stone from

Porthoustock with the stone loading shutes on the right.

Bodmin Moor; Gweek on the Helford River served Helston and local mines and quarries; Truro, Roundwood Quay, Pill Creek and Penryn on the Fal Estuary took minerals and stone from the Carnon Valley and Gwennap; on the River Tamar, Cotehele and Calstock exported minerals and stone from Gunnislake and the Tamar Valley mines; Forder and St German's Quay on the St German's River had extensive trade in stone from numerous local quarries. Other landing places included the extensive sand banks off Par taking cargoes of minerals and stone from the Luxulyan Valley; and the north Cornish 'porths' of Port Isaac and Port Gaverne which exported Delabole slate.

In the eighteenth and nineteenth centuries the industrial revolution caused a big increase of activity in Cornwall's mineral industries, and the county strived to satisfy the industrial world's insatiable demand for raw materials. A series of developments were undertaken to improve communications and harbour facilities.

In 1760 a pier was constructed at Portreath to improve the shipment of minerals; a basin was added in 1800 and nine years later the Portreath Tramroad was built to link the harbour with the mining district around Redruth. Improvements continued throughout the nineteenth century. There was a very long and narrow harbour entrance which restricted the size of ships. But the port served its purpose, exporting copper ore to Swansea for smelting and importing Welsh coal to fire the beam engines which drained the mines and powered other machinery.

A second development along the north coast was the establishment of a harbour in Trevaunance Cove, after several failed attempts. Named St Agnes Harbour, it served the St Agnes mining district. Clinging to the shore, below the cliffs, this exposed little harbour suffered constantly from gale damage. Once it had fallen out of use early in the twentieth century, the sea quickly demolished the protecting piers.

The third and most significant development on the north coast followed the establishment of a foundry by John Harvey in the Hayle River estuary during 1779. Harvey's Foundry became world famous for its pumping engines and other mining machinery. In 1818-9 the foundry company improved navigation of the Hayle River and built a quay for vessels of up to 150 tons to come alongside the Company's works. Opposition was forthcoming from the nearby Copperhouse Company, which built their own Copperhouse Quay. Both companies engaged in foundry work, shipped ore for smelting in south Wales and imported coal and timber for the mines, although Harvey's competitor failed in the 1860s. Harvey's also owned their own merchant fleet and after 1831 ran a steam packet service to Bristol – later linking with the new Great Western Railway from London.

Following a decline in the mining boom during the second half of the nineteenth century, Harvey's concentrated on shipbuilding and foundry work, being the only significant builder of iron ships in Cornwall. The foundry and shipyard closed in 1904, although the name survived until recent years, trading as builders merchants.

Although lacking natural sites for harbour development, the north Cornwall coast attracted proposals

Hayle

because of its proximity to the smelting works and coal mines of south Wales, whilst avoiding the longer and more hazardous alternative of a voyage around Land's End. However, the majority of Cornwall's maritime trade was on the south coast, with many sheltered potential locations for quays and, generally, shorter and easier transport from the mines to navigable water.

For instance, in 1826, a major mineral quay development was undertaken, not on an exposed coastal site, but tucked away in what today is a quiet backwater of the Fal Estuary. In 1826 the Redruth & Chasewater Railway Company selected a waterside site at Devoran, near the head of Restronguet Creek, to serve as terminus and wharves for its 4ft gauge mineral tramway which ran through the Redruth, Gwennap, St Day and Carnon Valley mining districts. Restronguet Creek already supported a smelting works at Point and a foundry at Perranarworthal. As the new wharves developed they drew trade away from the older mineral quays at nearby Roundwood Quay and Pill Creek. Sail traders and steamships visited Devoran's wharves, which grew to a considerable size. Silting always proved a problem, only partially solved by a reservoir sluice which scoured the channel, and paddle tugs which assisted the merchant ships. However, the quays survived the test of time, only falling into disrepair after closure of the railway in 1915.

The improvement in the construction of roads, particularly following the introduction of motor transport, called for the supply of stone chippings. One of the most spectacular of these roadstone quarries is at Porthoustock, where the cliff itself has been quarried away. River barges collected their cargoes of stone at Porthoustock by sailing under the loading chute jetties, which still dominate the shoreline. One of the main destinations on the Fal Estuary was Cornwall County Council's Highways depot at Tresillian, the highest navigable point on the estuary. River barges continued in this trade for some years after the Second World War. Similar quarries at Penlee in Mounts Bay were served by a narrow gauge railway, carrying the stone to Newlyn's South Pier. St Ives' West Pier was similarly given over to serve nearby quarries.

Narabo Wharf, Devoran with ore storage bins on the left.

Another stronghold of the roadstone trade was the estuary of the River Lynher and River Tiddy in east Cornwall where, well into the second half of the twentieth century, Thames spritsail barges and Dutch motor coasters were numbered amongst the vessels plying these idyllic waters to take out stone from Poldrissick, Treluggan and Forder Quays.

33

RESTRONGUET CREEK. Yard Point, just inside the mouth of the creek, was the location for the shipyard of John Stephens, where he and his shipwright, Peter Ferris, built schooners and ketches.

Point, in Penpoll Creek, was an industrialised area, with busy wharves and a tin smelting works.

Devoran was developed by the Redruth & Chasewater Railway Company in 1824, to serve their 4 ft gauge mineral railway. The wharves at Devoran grew into a substantial riverside port, but were plagued by silting problems throughout their history. The wharves fell into disuse once the railway closed in 1915. Their remains can still be seen in this, now silent backwater, with extensive stonebuilt ore storage bins and massive granite bollards along the line or the quay.

At Perran Wharf Welsh coal and Scandinavian timber (after which the nearby Norway Inn was, reputedly, named) was imported for the nearby mining districts. In 1791 the Perran Foundry was established by the Fox family of Falmouth. The Foundry buildings were converted to a mill in 1897.

PORTREATH. An ancient fishing port, the harbour at Portreath was developed to serve the mining industry. The artificial harbour was built during the second half of the eighteenth century chiefly for trade with south Wales. The harbour was leased to Fox & Co of Falmouth who improved facilities and built a new basin. An inner basin was constructed in 1846. In 1809 the Portreath tramroad, the first railway in Cornwall, was built, linking Portreath to the St Day and Gwennap mining districts.

Fishing continued and a considerable general trade was attracted. D. W. Bain & Co of Portreath

The tug PERRAN in Restronguet Creek

maintained a fleet of trading schooners, numbering 16 vessels in 1880.

Many of the harbours of the north coast have difficult entrances, but none can match Portreath. A ship had to make its way into the narrow entrance between the pier and a cliff face to the east. Then it had to negotiate the length of the channel up to the inner basin. No mean feat, particularly in the days of sail, when vessels often had to be warped up the channel. Trade declined considerably after the Second World War, and eventually ceased in the 1960s. The old quays, once piled high with ore and coal, were sold off for a housing development.

ST AGNES. There have been five attempts to construct an artificial harbour at St Agnes. John Tonkin started in 1632 to construct a 'peer or key' to serve trading vessels. His efforts were destroyed in gales during the following winter. A second attempt, by Hugh Tonkin in, 1684, was again destroyed by the sea. Hugh Tonkin's pier of 1699, built with the aid of Henry Winstanley, lasted until it was swept away by the sea in 1705. Thomas Tonkin completed the fourth harbour works in 1710. It was destroyed in 1736. In 1793 mining adventurers constructed a new harbour at the foot of the cliffs in Trevaunance Cove. Wooden staging on the cliffs above served as loading platforms, cargoes being lifted or lowered to the boats' holds by horse windlass. Ore was loaded by chute similar to those at Porthoustock

M. T. Hitchens & Co built schooners at St Agnes and maintained their own fleet. There were also some local fishing boats. The harbour continued to function until the 1920s. Since then its piers have been washed away, apart from the foundation courses which can be seen at low tide below the cliff to the west, on the boulder strewn shore; this is all that remains as evidence of the harbour.

NEWQUAY. A stone pier existed in the fifteenth century for the convenience of ships prevented by weather from entering the rivers Gannel or Porth – either side of this pier. By the end of the sixteenth century a 'new quay' was being built to replace the old pier, offering a harbour of refuge rather than trading facilities for what was no more than a small hamlet. Later the local communities supported pilchard seines and curing cellars

In 1833 Richard Lomax completed a harbour development which enclosed four acres. Five years later J. T. Austen acquired the harbour and developed it for the export of minerals and china clay. In 1849 a railway linked Newquay to the clay district.

The SS ISLEMAN entering Portreath

Four shipyards built schooners, ketches etc. and Newquay became an important shipowning centre. About 150 trading vessels were owned at the peak of the harbour's activity. From the 1870s trade began to dwindle. The last outward cargo left the port in 1921. The final inward cargo – manure – was landed by the schooner *Hobah* in 1922.

The stone jetty in the centre of Newquay Harbour dates from 1870. The railway once emerged from a short tunnel in the cliffs on a wooden bridge (now removed) and out on to the stone jetty now isolated in the middle of the harbour. Rails also ran onto the protecting outer pier. A second pier enclosed the harbour. By 1868 lodging houses for visitors to the spectacular beach scenery of Fistral and Newquay bays, already existed and the holiday trade has been Newquay's major industry ever since.

Newquay's Rowing Club have a number of pilot gigs, now used in the summer for racing. These include the *Newquay* built by Peters of St Mawes in 1812 and the *Dove* of 1820, as well as some built in the 1970s as a result of the revival of gig racing.

On the cliff road, near the Atlantic Hotel, is the curious little Huer's House, a lookout for the seine fishery, where a watchman was stationed to spot the approaching pilchard shoals.

PORT ISAAC. There was a pilchard fishery at Port Isaac before the sixteenth century. A protective stone pier was built during the Tudor period and its remains are still visible on the northern shore, inside the post-Great War breakwaters.

In 1850 there were 49 fishing boats registered and 4 fish cellars. The large fish cellars in the south corner of the cove were built in the nineteenth century and continue to be used by the fishing fleet. The sheds under the Pentus wall, in the northern corner of the cove, were built for storing fishing tackle. Roofing slate from the nearby Delabole quarries was shipped out from the beach. There were two boat building yards in Port Isaac, adjacent to the fish cellars.

A small coasting trade developed from the slate shipping activity. Ketches and smacks of 50 to 80 tons were built and owned in Port Isaac and traded mainly in the Irish Sea.

The old lifeboat station, now the village post office, was established in 1869. The lifeboat had to be wheeled through the narrow streets on a carriage. A new station was opened in 1927, at the top of the beach and slipway. It was closed just six years later, but the boathouse still stands. An inshore lifeboat was introduced in 1967. The lifeboat is housed inside the fish cellars.

Port Issac with fish cellars on the right.

William Cookworthy, a Plymouth chemist, searched geologically suitable areas in the west country for the materials needed in the production of Chinese-style porcelain, the manufacture of which had remained a secret for centuries. He discovered deposits of Kaolin or china-clay, as it became known, in west Cornwall and then, in the St Austell district, he not only discovered a suitable supply, but seemingly inexhaustible deposits of the finest china clay in the world. By the 1780s he had established his own porcelain manufactory in Plymouth. The mining and quarrying of this clay was to transform the landscape of central Cornwall and initiate the development of some of the most substantial and longest lasting of all Cornwall's harbours built during the Industrial Revolution.

Ships took china clay out from the beaches at Porthpean, Pentewan, West Polmear and Par, for St Austell Bay had no natural harbour. But such landings were severely disrupted by storms, especially during the winter months. By 1800 production had reached 2000 tons a year and with an ever increasing demand from the Staffordshire potteries for china clay, a series of harbour developments in St Austell Bay resulted.

Subsequent to three ships being lost at West Polmear in 1790, the local landowner, Charles Rashleigh, began the construction of a pier the next year. Based on the engineer John Smeaton's concept, during the next seven years the excavation of an inner basin took place, protected by lock gates and an outer basin. Warehouses and dwellings, hotel, ropewalk, fish cellars and a boat-building yard completed the new community, the population of which increased from 9 to 900 during the next decade. West Polmear became Charlestown.

A quarter of a century later a second harbour development was nearing completion. Since 1744 the Hawkins family had established harbour facilities at Pentewan, about three miles south of Charlestown, near the mouth of the St Austell River. By the turn of the century these harbour works were derelict and shipping had reverted to beach landings. In 1817 Sir Charles Hawkins entered into an agreement for the construction of a new harbour on the site. The work was completed in 1826 and linked to St Austell by a horse tramway three years later. The bulk of the china clay traffic was diverted through the streets of St Austell to reach the new harbours. By 1830 the town had

Charlestown c1920s

become seriously congested with clay wagons and a third harbour scheme was promoted in St Austell Bay. Although initially intended to export granite and copper ore, Par Harbour later outgrew its two neighbours in the china clay trade. This artificial harbour was promoted and financed by Joseph Thomas Austen of Fowey, to serve his Luxulyan Valley quarries and Fowey Consols mine. Construction work commenced in 1829 on the open beach at Par. By 1840 a 1200ft breakwater and pier enclosed 35 acres. A two mile canal was built alongside the Luxulyan

Pentewan

River, from Par to Pontsmill. From the canal terminus an incline plane served Fowey Consols mine, while a seven mile tramroad to the granite quarries on Molinnis Moors reached the north east edge of the china clay district.

Contemporary with the Par development was a scheme to provide harbour facilities at Newquay, (on the north coast) which was then nothing more than a small fishing hamlet – its 'New' quay dating from the sixteenth century. In 1833 Richard Lomax completed work on the harbour piers which enclosed an area of four acres and was accessible to vessels up to 700 tons at all states of the tide. In 1838 Joseph Thomas Treffry (Austen had changed his name to that of his mother's, co-heiress of the Treffrys of Fowey) purchased Newquay Harbour from Lomax, further extended it and, in 1844, obtained an Act of Parliament to build a railway from Newquay into the china clay district.

But Pentewan was soon struggling to survive. The valleys of the St Austell River and its tributaries passed through stream works and the china clay district, silt from which was choking the harbour entrance adjacent to the mouth of the river.

All of the above ventures were artificial harbours, constructed as near as possible to the clay and mining districts. The nearest natural harbour was the deep water estuary of the Fowey River and the introduction of steam railways in the mid-nineteenth century finally rendered Fowey's vast natural resource within reach of the mineral and clay districts. In Caffa Mill Pill, immediately upstream from Fowey, J. T. Treffry had built a small dock because, prior to his Par scheme, he had contemplated building a railway from his mines to Carne Point, near Caffa Mill Pill. A railway line was again projected in 1861 and eventually built and opened from Lostwithiel in 1869. Five years later the Cornwall Minerals Railway opened a line from Par to Fowey. Its primary objective was to ship an expected 1,000 tons of iron ore per day from Fowey Harbour. These two railways also provided Fowey with a direct connection to the china clay district.

The iron ore traffic failed to materialise, but the Cornwall Minerals Railway survived on the clay trade and introduced hydraulic wagon tipping frames, for loading clay into the ships' holds. The Great Western Railway took over in 1876 and developed the facilities at Fowey, especially after the turn of the century.

The relative importance to the china clay trade of these harbours, might be gauged by noting the clay shipments from each in 1858:

Charlestown/Pentewan	64,845 tons
Par	15,154 tons
Newquay	2,788 tons
Truro	150 tons
Padstow	25 tons
others	150 tons

Fowey's deep water berths served ocean going shipping from the United States, Canada, Russia and the Baltic countries etc. While Par and Charlestown catered for smaller vessels in the coastal and Home Trades (i.e. Germany, Netherlands, Belgium and France). Meanwhile, Pentewan's silting problems continued. In 1877 steam locomotives were introduced on the harbour's mineral line, greatly improving communication with St Austell. But horse drawn wagons, in even greater numbers, still needed to

In the last quarter of the nineteenth century exports from Fowey, Par and Charlestown exceeded all other clay ports by a huge margin.

Clay shipped in 1885:

Fowey	114,403 tons
Par	86,325 tons
Charlestown	59,690 tons
Pentewan	24,960 tons
Newquay	4,152tons
Penzance	1,570 tons
Padstow/Wadebridge	1,475 tons
Penryn	1,024 tons
Porthleven	860 tons
Hayle	390 tons

negotiate St Austell's streets to reach the railway's terminus, as they also had to for Charlestown. Silting of Pentewan's harbour mouth remained a major problem and all attempted solutions failed, or even made matters worse. Pentewan continued in slow decline until the railway equipment was requisitioned during the Great War. The harbour changed hands in 1918 and a new trade flourished briefly – the supply of building sand, for which the silt clogging the harbour proved admirable. The last clay cargo left the harbour in 1929 – although this was something of a one off event. The last trading vessels called in 1940 for cargoes of cement or concrete blocks.

The trade at Charlestown continued steadily despite its disadvantages in horse wagon days, and the severe limit to shipping resulting from the constricted entrance. New lock gates were fitted in 1971. The number of vessels visiting the harbour in 1980 was 144, taking out 61,000 tons of clay, mostly for the independent Goonvean and Rostowrack China Clay Co, a figure little changed since 1885. The harbour and village remained in the ownership of one family for about 160 years, and little has changed in that time. Following the sale of Charlestown in 1986 the harbour has been closed to china clay ships.

Clay now arrives by road or rail or in liquid form by pipeline, at Par which remains the main harbour for small European motor coasters, while Fowey can handle ships of about 12,000 tons, and in 1986 handled 1.6 million tons of cargo, almost all of it china clay.

RIVER FOWEY CLAY WHARVES. A series of river quays occupy the western bank of the River Fowey, opposite St Winnow, at Golant and below Colvithick Wood. These riverside quays have largely been isolated from the farming communities they once served, by the railway which runs along the shoreline from Lostwithiel to the clay wharves and loading jetties opposite Mixtow and Bodinnick. The clay wharves of Fowey and the harbour of Par are linked by a private road – the former trackbed of the Cornwall Minerals Railway.

Clay, brought down by train, is loaded directly into the holds of ships in a highly mechanised and efficient way, using the latest technology. These busy clay wharves are mostly hidden from view from Fowey itself, but it is an impressive sight to see ships, some over 10,000 tons, slowly pass by only yards from Fowey's Town Quay. The best viewpoints are gained from the shoreline around Mixtow or, even better, by boat. A number of small motor boats are available for hire from Town Quay.

River Fowey clay wharves c.1910.
COURTESY MICHAEL MESSENGER

PAR. The tide once reached St Blazey, where a bridge crossed the Luxulyan River. A ferry crossed the estuary at Par at high tide. Silt, generated by tin streaming, choked the narrow estuary and by the end of the nineteenth century the sea had receded. Ships beached on the extensive sandbanks near Par to load minerals. Granite for both Rudyeard's and Smeaton's Eddystone Lighthouses were loaded in this way.

Developed by J. T. Treffry to serve his mines and

Par Harbour in the 1930s

quarries, Par Harbour was reclaimed from the sand banks and completed in 1840. Intense industrial activity within the docks and around its immediate vicinity may still be witnessed, in terms of both extensive industrial remains and the continuing importance of the harbour in the clay trade. Original installations included a lead smelting works, brickworks, pilchard fishery, shipbuilding yard, granite dressing yard and a candle factory – for the mining industry.

Par became a shipbuilding and shipowning community, building schooners for the Newfoundland and Home trades. Benjamin Tregaskes maintained one of the last wooden ship repair yards in the country, catering for the rapidly declining fleet of coastal ketches and schooners in the twentieth century. In the nineteenth century though, some ten schooners and barquentines of

up to 250 tons were built there. The dry dock, the only one between Falmouth and Plymouth continued in use until 1957. The renowned ship portrait painter Rueben Chappel was also based at Par, painting steam coasters and Britain's last sail trading vessels.

CHARLESTOWN. Charlestown was developed by Charles Rashleigh, a local landowner and mining adventurer. In 1791 he began excavations in the cove of West Polmear, where trading vessels took the beach to discharge and load cargoes. The works were completed in 1801, to the plan of John Smeaton, specially designed to transport copper ore from nearby mines, Soon, however, china cay was to become the dominant trade of the port. The present cobbled car park areas were storage areas for copper and china clay. Much else remains of this late eighteenth century harbour

CHINA CLAY PROCESSING AND LOADING ARRANGEMENT AT CHARLESTOWN

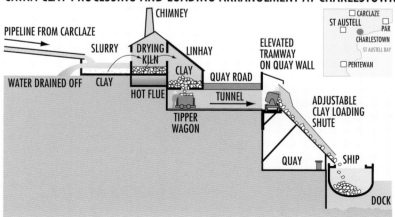

Charlestown in 1984

spectacular scene, which itself is regularly transformed as a living set for numerous film productions. Amongst the wreck exhibits in the Shipwreck Centre are to be found items of the villages own maritime history.

PENTEWAN. Another clay and minerals harbour, developed in the nineteenth century, Pentewan was built by the local landowner Sir Charles Hawkins. It was opened in 1826 and within three years a tramway was built to link the harbour with St Austell. The narrow gauge line was converted to steam traction in 1872.

village including the hexagonal harbour office overlooking the outer basin. In addition there was a shipyard, ropewalk, pilchard fishery, warehouses limekiln, brickworks – indeed everything needed in a self-sufficient maritime community.

Dry clay from the storage linhays, like the large building behind the Shipwreck Centre was carried by a tramway beneath the quay road to the loading chutes. Similar chutes in evidence today were designed to work from road level. The lower quay, on the west side, was chiefly for unloading coal and cask staves from the Baltic at a time when much china clay was exported in barrels.

Since the sale of the village in 1986, the harbour has closed as a china clay port, and has become the base for Traditional Sail, which provides sailing craft for film and television. The harbour and its collection of period sailing vessels present a

Plagued throughout its life with silting problems in the harbour mouth, Pentewan effectively lost its clay traffic after 1919. The last trading vessels called for sand and concrete cargoes in the 1940s. However, the dock remains intact, with water in the basin. The lock gates and winches are still in situ as are many dockside buildings including the Harbourmaster's house, weighbridge and stores. Beyond the lock gates towards the sea, Pentewan's silting problem is plainly evident. The channel, jetty and breakwater are virtually buried beneath sand, which has built up for many years. Rails laid along the outer jetty owe their existence to a concrete block and sand works which was established after the Great War.

Charlestown 2002

Pentewan Harbour c1910

40

It is perhaps with its fishing villages and rugged coastline that Cornwall's maritime heritage is most closely associated, but at intervals the granite cliffs break rank and the sea spills inland to fill the estuaries of the Tamar, Looe, Fowey, Fal, Helford and Camel Rivers. Prior to the advent of railways such tidal estuaries were invaluable to the trade and development of their waterside communities. A glance at the map of Cornwall offers evidence of this importance. Saltash, Looe, Fowey, Loswithiel, Falmouth, Penryn, Truro, Padstow and Wadebridge each owe their existence to the river estuary upon which they grew. The coastal and deep sea trades which such ports supported are described elsewhere in this book.

Upon each of Cornwall's navigable estuaries there evolved local 'inside trades', ranging from simple drifting lighters on the River Camel, to large sailing barge fleets on the rivers Tamar and Fal. Small rowing boat ferries provided passage across the narrower stretches of rivers. Large steamboat fleets offered passenger communication between a number of river quays – these were the maritime lorries and buses, as it were, usually working to the very limit of salt water to serve the estuarine communities and industries of Cornwall.

The river traffic varied on each estuary, dependent upon the landbased industries, size of population and the nature of the estuary itself. In the Tamar Valley an ideal environment for fruit and vegetable growing was matched at the river's mouth by the hungry population of the 'Three Towns' of Plymouth, Devonport and Stonehouse – the largest centre of population on the south coast of England. In addition, the Tamar Valley became an area of mining and industrial activity. Thus there grew a large fleet of river barges, to carry manure and supplies up-river and agricultural, mineral, and industrial produce down.

On the Tamar and Fal estuaries a large number of river barges worked the quiet backwaters to lonely quays. Many of these barges were owned and manned by the same agricultural communities they were built to serve. Inside barges were usually smack rigged, carrying a huge mainsail to catch the slightest breeze in the sheltered estuaries. When the elements conspired against the bargeman,

A river barge at Percuil on the Fal Estuary

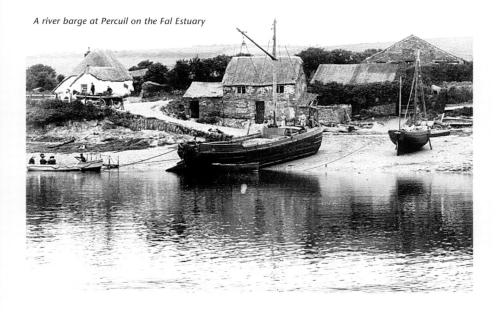

long sweeps (oars) or quant poles (like punting poles) were brought into use. Fully laden these barges could sail with just two inches of freeboard. They had very strong hulls for taking the ground at uneven mud berths. Barge builders included Emmanuel Crocker of Gunnislake, James Goss of Calstock, George Westcott and George Fisher of Saltash, Charles Burt of Falmouth, William Scoble and John Davies of Malpas and Charles Dyer of Sunny Corner, Truro. In addition to its river barges, the Port of Truro also supported a fleet of river lighters, traditionally maintained by the waterside community of Cowland Creek. These served ships with too deep a draught to reach Truro fully laden. River barges called at farm quays such as Buttspill, Terrace Meadows and Collogget on the Tamar estuary, and Pollingey, Cowlands and Trewince on the Fal. Agricultural trade was also established at river ferry crossings such as Halton Quay, Cargreen, or Percuil owing in the main to their long established accessibility from both the river and the surrounding farmland. Motor road transport eventually killed

A river barge sailing past King Harry Ferry on the River Fal.

off the river barge trade, although a few survived into the 1950s – ironically carrying roadstone from quarries in the St Germans River estuary and Porthoustock, where they held out until quarries closed or nearby roads were improved.

CORNISH RIVER QUAYS OF THE TAMAR ESTUARY

CALSTOCK. Once a busy inland shipowning centre and seaport, until local mines declined in the last half of the nineteenth century. Calstock was frequented by schooners, ketches and barges, in the home, coastal and local trades – and by steam coasters taking out granite from Pearson's quarry in Gunnislake. The arrival of rail communication in 1907 and the advent of motor transport during the 1920s finally won its remaining agricultural trade. The most prominent feature is the railway viaduct, built of concrete blocks. A steam powered wagon hoist, located on the western side of the viaduct at the Calstock end, lowered granite wagons to the quayside: the hoist was removed in the 1930s. Sections of Calstock's old quay walls remain, as do some older quayside buildings. Parts of the house immediately upstream of the viaduct once served as the office of the Devon & Cornwall Steam Packet Co Ltd, which operated paddle steamers on the River Tamar, including the 110ft *Empress*

which served as a market boat between Calstock and Devonport until 1925.

Although generally referred to as Calstock, on the opposite bank of the river and therefore in Devon can be seen the site of James Goss' boatyard. On the flat land in front of Ferry Farm, formerly the Ferryboat Inn, many fine small ketch rigged barges were built, culminating in the *Garlandstone*, completed in 1907, and now to be seen at Morwellham Quay where she is undergoing restoration. A model of the Goss yard can be seen in the museum at Cotehele Quay.

COTEHELE QUAY. Owned by the National Trust, Cotehele Quay served the Mount Edgcumbe family's Cotehele House and estate. The quays, limekilns and buildings are carefully maintained. A small maritime museum, depicting the shipping and trade of the River Tamar, has been established by the National Maritime Museum on the ground floor of a quayside warehouse. Also maintained

CALSTOCK. General View I.

Calstock with the Tamar paddle steamer ALEXANDRA headed downstream.

and moored at the quay is the Tamar sailing barge *Shamrock*, which was built by Frederick Hawke of Stonehouse in 1899. She worked the river until 1919 and then spent 42 years in the stone trade, first based on the Lynher river and then working between Porthoustock on the Lizard and Cornwall County Council's roadstone depot at Tresillian, on the Fal estuary. Similar vessels working to quays like Cotehele carried supplies of the notorious 'dock dung' or 'night soil' from Devonport's Pottery Quay, for manuring the Tamar Valley's market gardens.

HALTON QUAY. Halton Quay was the distribution point for market garden produce of the St Dominick area. It was leased to the Plymouth Co-operative Society and served by their own fleet of river barges. Lime kilns and the attractive quay office remain, the latter now a small chapel. The grass embankment on the foreshore is not the original quayside, but remains of the quay can still be viewed at low tide, almost covered in riverbank mud.

CARGREEN. The main street of the village ends abruptly at the waters edge. Coastal trading vessels and local barges called at the two sided quay, designed to offer shelter against the action of the tide and river flow. It is difficult to imagine that this quiet village once warranted a revenue cutter to control its smuggling activities.

KINGSMILL LAKE. A beautiful and tranquil creek, immediately upstream from Saltash. A series of picturesque quays, Landulph, Pineapple, Moditonham and Cologget served the market garden community of the Botus Fleming district. The tiny Moditonham Quay survives intact, with public access, and represents a typical example of the Tamar Valley's agricultural quays, which were once the lifeblood of Tamar barges like *Shamrock*.

THE RIVERS LYNHER & TIDDY. Quays and landings on the combined estuary of the two

Halton Quay and the former quay office of Plymouth Co-operative Society.

43

St Germans Quay

rivers included Antony Passage, from where a passenger ferry crossed to Jupiter Point on the Antony shore and Jessops' Quarry quay in Forder Lake (creek), which was served by Jessops' own river barges. Wacker Quay, on the southern shore, was used by the War Department to land supplies and ordnance for Screasdon and Tregantle Forts and remains of the military railway can still be detected at the quay.

Treluggan and Poldrissick Quays on the River Lynher were busy in the 'blue elvan' roadstone trade until the 1950s frequented by Tamar barges, ketches, schooners and later by Dutch motor coasters. The hulks of the schooner *Millom Castle* – one of the last trading vessels to discharge at Cargreen – and the river barge *Lynher* were to be seen quietly rotting away at Poldrissick – the barge *Lynher* has subsequently been rescued, rebuilt and

Moditonham Quay in Kingsmill Lake, on the Tamar Estuary near Saltash.

can sometimes be seen sailing her home waters. The River Lynher was navigable to Notter Quay, just upstream from the present A38 road bridge.

The tributary River Tiddy joins the Lynher below St Germans Quay – which lies on the western bank of the Tiddy, below the railway viaduct, and is the most important quay on the two rivers. The combined estuary, from the mouth at Antony to St Germans Quay is thus known as the St Germans River. Once an important trading place for stone and minerals from Caradon and market gardens in the St Germans district (with produce destined for Saltash and later Devonport), the large quay, warehouse and quayside cottages all remain in their beautiful setting. The Tiddy was navigable for small barges right up to Morva and Kilna Quays in Tideford.

MILLBROOK LAKE. Quays at Southdown date from 1650, when a gunpowder works was established and the 1730s, when the King's Brewhouse was built. Beer rather than water was supplied on Naval ships at the time, due to its superior keeping qualities and 20,000 gallons a week could brewed here to supply the Devonport-based fleet. At Foss, local passenger boats are repaired alongside the tide mill building which was once owned by miller John Parsons, who founded the Millbrook Steamboat Company in 1900. The playing field now located behind the mill building was the mill pond. At Millbrook, storehouses and limekilns once sited at the waters edge, are now stranded inland as a result of infilling schemes. At the end of Molesworth Terrace there stood two piers, each used by opposing Millbrook and Saltash based steamboat companies which competed vigorously for the lucrative passenger trade between Millbrook Lake and Devonport.

At Anderton, on a small point of land, are the remains of a boatbuilding yard where James and John Waterman once built wooden vessels. In the 1880s they moved their business to Cremyll.

Note: Most creeks within the Port of Plymouth are known as 'lakes'.

The preserved Tamar barge SHAMROCK
COURTESY RICHARD CLAMMER

Millbrook Lake

FERRIES

Ferries have long crossed Cornwall's rivers at convenient points. The right to operate the earliest ferries was granted to respective landowners by the sovereign of the day. The Saltash Ferry was owned by the Valletort family after the Norman Conquest. In the fourteenth century it was bestowed to the Mayor and Burgesses of Saltash. The Earls of Mount Edgcumbe maintained the Cremyll Ferry until they sold the rights in 1946. The Flushing Ferry in Falmouth Harbour was granted by Charles II to Sir Peter Killigrew in 1660. On the Helford River, the Manor of Merthen held the rights to the Helford Ferry. The Percuil Ferry on the Fal estuary was an example of an ecclesiastical ferry, being owned by the Bishops of Sherborne until it passed to the Bishop of Exeter in the tenth century and the Church Commissioners in 1835. On the River Camel the Padstow to Rock ferry dates back to the creation of the Duchy in 1337.

Some ancient ferries offered an indispensable river crossing on the main routes through the county. Their importance can be judged by the number which still operate. The Cremyll Ferry at the mouth of the Tamar has operated since time immemorable and still provides a year round ferry crossing. The Saltash Ferry closed in 1961, replaced by the suspension bridge. On the River Fowey both the Polruan pedestrian ferry and the Bodinnick vehicular ferry date back to the 1300s and still operate year round. Two ancient crossings remain on the Fal, the Flushing pedestrian ferry and the King Harry vehicular ferry.

Communities and other convenient crossing places have also been served periodically by ferries or steamer services which were established as circumstances demanded. The Rumleigh ferry on the Tamar linked Calstock and the Okel Tor Mine to Gawton Mine and Rumleigh Brickworks on the Bere Alston peninsula. The Mylor–Greatwood ferry on the Fal estuary survived for as long as the Naval Dockyard at Mylor existed. On the River Gannel the Fern Pit and Crantock ferries were established in the nineteenth century to serve visitors wishing to cross the river when the tide was in. Saltash, Torpoint and Millbrook steamboat services provided important services on the Hamoaze, gradually fading out with the growth of motor transport. Some major crossings which were established in the eighteenth and nineteenth centuries remain important today. The Torpoint Ferry is the largest vehicular river ferry operating in Britain and the St Mawes passenger boat service, which links the one time fishing village to Falmouth, is as busy today as it ever was.

Malpas Ferry, R. Fal

Argall's Series.

Malpas Ferry c1900

One of the three floating bridges of the Torpoint Ferry

TORPOINT FERRY. Developed during the late eighteenth century by the Carew family of Antony, Torpoint served as a graving beach for naval and other ships. Here ships were careened (beached) for maintenance, re-caulking and tarring (thus Tar Point). A substantially built ballast pond from this period is a prominent feature of the foreshore. Merchant ships sailing light (with spare capacity or a light cargo), and Naval vessels without full provisions and ordnance, required ballast – stone, scrap etc – to achieve their correct sailing draft. Ballast could be discharged or loaded at the ballast pond, which today provides moorings for boats.

A turnpike road from Torpoint was built to link with the older Saltash to Cremyll road and in 1791 the newly established Torpoint Ferry gained the Cornish mail contract from the much older Cremyll Ferry, at the mouth of the Tamar. The familiar floating bridge had yet to be established and horse and passenger boats landed at New Passage and North Corner respectively, on the Devon shore. The first floating bridge was introduced in 1834, designed by James Rendel – having established a similar floating bridge at Saltash in the previous year. The floating bridges of the Torpoint Ferry now number three and a service is maintained 24 hours a day and 365 days a year. Whilst the suspension bridge at Saltash is the principal route into Cornwall, the south eastern corner of Cornwall continues to offer desirable homes for many working in the Plymouth district and the future of the Torpoint Ferry is thus secured – there is no viable alternative.

Both the outlook and a distinctly naval atmosphere along the Torpoint foreshore bear witness to the town's close association with the Devonport Dockyard on the opposite shore. *HMS Fisgard*, the Royal Navy training base, is located on the outskirts of Torpoint. The firing range of the base occupies a part of the shoreline along the adjacent wide, but shallow, St John's Lake.

CREMYLL FERRY. Since the 1930s Mashford (once of Saltash) have occupied the boatyards and slipways, where the Waterman brothers and Rogers & Co (Shipbuilding) Ltd once built boats for the Navy, Devonport Dockyard and the local maritime communities. The Cremyll Ferry runs from Cremyll Quay to Admiral's Hard, in Stonehouse. This ancient ferry belonged to the Mount Edgcumbe Estate until sold to the Millbrook Steamboat & Trading Co. Ltd in 1946. The diesel engined *Northern Belle*, which currently maintains the service, has been doing so for nearly 80 years, since she was built as the steamboat *Armadillo* by Rogers in 1926.

Cremyll Quay, which was developed for the Mount Edgcumbe Estate by James Rendel in 1836, additionally served as a landing for vessels trading to the estate.

KING HARRY FERRY & TOLVERNE REACHES OF THE RIVER FAL. Turnaware Point, King Harry Ferry and Tolverne Cottage each provide excellent viewpoints for these stretches of the river. The King Harry Ferry is an ancient crossing. The first floating bridge was introduced in 1889. There have been six floating bridges – three steam and three diesel. The current bridge was built in 1974 by Dredge Marine of Ponsharden.

As times this crossing provides spectacular views

The NORTHERN BELLE on the Cremyll Ferry in 2002.

King Harry Ferry

The Miranda on the Flushing Ferry

of ocean going shipping laid up in the King Harry and Tolverne reaches. A visit to Tolverne Smugglers Cottage restaurant will offer views of Tolverne Reach, while inside the cottage is a virtual museum of memorabilia from ships that have been laid-up in the Fal.

FLUSHING FERRY. The Flushing Ferry runs from Old Quay. Since the seventeenth century at least, this ferry ran to Greenbank Quay, directly opposite, but following the introduction of steamboats in the 1870s, the opportunity was taken to alter the route to land at Market Strand, nearer the centre of Falmouth.

River Fal Steamship Co Ltd's Victoria

HELFORD FERRY. Runs from the Ferry Boat Inn at Helford Passage. Originally it was an ecclesiastic ferry, belonging to the Bishop of Exeter but was sold to the local landowner Tyack of Merthen Manor and leased to boatmen.

RIVER STEAMBOAT COMPANIES. The estuaries of the Fal and Tamar rivers once supported large river steamer fleets. On the Fal deep draught tug-like screw steamers of the River Fal Steamship Co Ltd linked Truro to Falmouth, while the St Mawes Steam Tug & Passenger Co Ltd was based around their mail-steamer service across the Carrick Roads to St Mawes and Percuil. Both companies ran seasonal excursions from Falmouth's Prince of Wales Pier. The shallow rivers and creeks of the Tamar estuary called for shallow draught paddle steamers. These were based in Calstock, Saltash and Millbrook linking east Cornwall and the Tamar Valley to Devonport. Principal fleets were the Saltash, Three Towns & District Steamboat Co Ltd and the Millbrook Steamboat Company.

The Rock Ferry leaving Padstow, with Rock across the River Camel in the background.

BEACH TRADING

There are not many coves or beaches along the Cornish coast that have not witnessed some maritime activity. Fishing and trading vessels utilised many such places which had reasonable access from the land. The coast is littered with these trading places or 'Porths', where small sailing vessels came in, and were run aground near high tide. As the tide ebbed, they could be unloaded ready to float off on the next high tide preferably with the help of a wind off the land. Some later developed into harbours, but the beaching of small boats continues at smaller fishing coves like Penberth, where a windlass survives which formerly hauled boats up the steep beach to safety.

Coasting schooners, ketches and trading smacks 'took the beach' at these porths to discharge coal, salt, manure and general supplies. Exports, depending upon the location, included fish, stone, slate, minerals and agricultural produce. Beach trading developed before many of the later harbours were built. At Pentewan, West Polmear and Par, for instance, ships were calling at the beaches to take out minerals long before the eighteenth century clay ports of St Austell Bay were constructed.

This sometimes risky trade, which called for an intimate knowledge of the coast's weather and sea conditions, continued well into the twentieth century. Wherever a cargo awaited collection at an isolated cove, it rendered the delivery of coal or lime profitable for small trading vessels. The beach trade only survived because it helped to extend the useful life of ageing ketches and smacks, although their insurance clubs set strict conditions, usually restricting their calls from April to September. The trading vessels needed to be strongly built. A constant watch was kept on the weather as carts were brought to the water's edge. Motor lorries inevitably won the majority of this trade. The beach trade faded out between the world wars, and the small trading vessels disappeared from the Cornish coast.

CANALS

Cornish canals are a rarity. Although various schemes were proposed in Cornwall during the 'Canal Age' (c. mid 1700s until the early 1800s), the geography of the county's river estuaries and harbours left few industrial ventures too far from maritime access. However, there were a few schemes that passed the planning stage:

TAMAR MANURE NAVIGATION. Completed in 1800 the Tamar Manure Navigation maintained a 5ft deep channel from the river port of Morwellham, on the Devon bank of the Tamar, to New Bridge at Gunnislake – a distance of some 3 miles further inland than barges would previously have been able to navigate on a regular basis. A cut (the only canal looking stretch of the navigation) measuring 600ft in length, bypassed the fish weir at Weir Head – the former limit of navigation. Together with the fish weir, which was increased in height, and a lock at the southern end of the cut, a 5ft channel above the weir was maintained to a quay at New Bridge. Initially it was hoped the navigation might link with the

Entrance to the lock gates of the Tamar Manure Navigation, downstream of Weir Head.

Bude Canal at Launceston – for what purpose seems obscure now (suggestions of ships thereby avoiding navigation around Land's End seem extremely optimistic). However, the navigation remained in isolation, but enjoyed a successful and surprisingly long life. Serving the Gunnislake district, a gasworks and brickworks, regular traffic included: manure (lime, sand, 'dock dung' and seaweed), coal, bricks and granite. The canal fell out of use after the Great War. The canal cut at Gunnislake is a Scheduled Ancient Monument.

BUDE. Bude was primarily an agricultural trading port, serving farming communities remote from any other port or major centre of population. The idea for a canal to trade inland was first mooted in 1770. In 1819 the Bude Harbour & Canal Company had plans for two canals approved, one to terminate near Launceston, the other near Holsworthy, in Devon. Lime bearing sea sand was transported inland, the sand being dug from the beach at Bude. A four foot gauge plateway, later a two foot gauge tramway, with man handled wagons, brought the sand to the canal quayside. Some of the tramway, near the sea lock gates in Bude, is still in location.

James Green, the engineer, favoured incline planes instead of locks, to link different canal levels. Canal barges with wheels, engaged rails on the inclines. The power to lift the barges came from counter-balance water weighted buckets in deep shafts, which were filled at the top and emptied at the bottom, once the barge had reached the summit.

Bude Canal sea lock and breakwater

At the entrance to the sea lock at Bude a protecting breakwater was built to safeguard shipping waiting to enter the canal. This was destroyed in 1828, but twelve years later the surviving breakwater was completed. Trading vessels transshipped cargoes onto the quay or into barges at the wharf alongside the broad reach of the canal inside the sea lock at Bude. After the railway arrived in Launceston, Holsworthy and then Bude itself, trade on the canal declined. In 1891 an Act was sought to abandon sections. In 1901 Bude-Stratton Urban District Council purchased the section of the canal at the Bude end for waterworks improvements. Two miles of the canal survive, used for leisure purposes. Bude-Stratton Museum is housed in a canalside warehouse, with many canal exhibits.

The canal and sea lock at Bude c 1910